# MINI-MANUAL OF
# *THE INDEPENDENT*
# *COUNTERTERRORIST*
## Third Edition

# R.J. GODLEWSKI

*Mini-Manual of the Independent Counterterrorist, Third Edition*

## DEDICATION

*To all who devote his or her life to defeating evil, wherever it may be found, and protecting innocent human lives wherever they may live.*

# TABLE OF CONTENTS

# INTRODUCTION TO THIRD EDITION

The need for personal safety and survival has evolved at an alarming rate. As these words are written, the United States is recovering from the aftermath of yet another shooting at the military installation at Fort Hood, Texas; the Russians are continuing to blackmail the Ukrainians into accepting their invasion and annexation of Crimea; an as of yet unsolved disappearance exists of a Malaysian airliner with 239 people aboard; and national debts soar at incalculable levels. These crises and a great many more conspire to place *the individual citizen* into harm's way with little or no recourse for their safety other than what he or she provides for themselves.

Understanding the need for citizen involvement within society's survival, *The Independent Counterterrorist* began as an online program to provide interested parties with the material needed to develop a *personal* training program to defeat anyone set against destroying human lives. During 2008, the first edition of *Mini-Manual of The Independent Counterterrorist* came within a very limited distribution channel. For a variety of reasons, it took four years for a second, "cleaner" version to become available through traditional book distributors and, thankfully, that particular edition has seen moderate success in North America and Europe. Nevertheless, events evolve at a greater pace than any single book – popular, academic, or otherwise – could hope to satisfy.

After some heavy thought and soul-searching, it has been determined that a new edition of *Mini-Manual* needs to be released. The basis for this decision rests upon the increasingly *martial* nature of transnational criminal organizations (TCO), drug trafficking organizations (DTO), and Islamic jihadists – all of whom now actively target American and Western interests, even from within the midst of our smallest towns and municipalities. Taxpayer-funded law enforcement agencies are shrinking and cannot hope to provide honorable citizens with a means to protect the innocent. Because of this, the *only* means of defeating these threats remains to "out insurgency, the insurgents" – in other words, to confront them with a sea of responsible citizens arising from within the communities under assault.

Therefore, the primary changes to the *Mini-Manual* within this edition remain twofold. First, a new discussion of the networked structure of criminal and terrorist groups will be presented. For instance, despite the proclivity for convenience in employing familiar terms, DTOs do not represent "cartels". In reality, they employ various daisy chain and wheel networks that interconnect solely on an as-needed basis. More often than not, these social structures change more frequently than other, traditionally bureaucratic organizations and may, depending upon the time or situation, either cooperate or compete with similar groups.

The second major change deals with the wide variety of equipment and resources available for the budding "independent" counterterrorist. In addition to the wide availability of firearms, communications technologies, body armor and clothing, etc., a responsible adult now has the opportunity to purchase *realistic* terrorist targets against which to practice. Remember, terrorists and criminals are becoming much more advanced in their tactics and equipment. So, too, must you or else you will quickly succumb to any confrontation. Again, you are *not* training to kill; you are *preparing* to defend. There remains a *significant* difference.

Terrorists and transnational criminal elements remain indiscriminate in nature. They will kill innocent women and children if it only serves their purpose. They will *not* bat an eyelash over the death of a newborn infant unless they can derive some measure of value from the atrocity. This is because all the threats aligned against you remain well versed in fourth-generation warfare (4GW) – the simultaneous engagement of martial, religious, political, and economic arenas in battle. For instance, terrorists may detonate a bomb on a crowded school bus and even claim that doing so served some ill-conceived religious devotion. Yet, if you somehow inadvertently injured a single child, *your* "atrocity" would be broadcast to the entire planet as proof positive that Americans, Westerners, Christians, or, perhaps even, Californians, remain evil people.

*Every* action that you take must be consciously reviewed in light of the four aspects of 4GW. That is, what religious (yes, folks, religion *matters* regardless of your personal beliefs), political, and economic ramifications are there to your protecting yourself and your family from martial threats? More importantly, how will *you* incorporate religious, political, and economic "weapons" into your overall martial package? These considerations warrant further – and continual – discussion and, accordingly, the need for a new edition of this book.

The future beckons crises of unimaginable proportions. We are steamrolling towards economic ruin, wars of ever-increasing ferocity, and – far worse – generations of apathetic youngsters whose concentration rests solely with the technology literally in his or her hand. Human individuals have, in the strongest implication of the argument, lost all concept of *humanity*. We have already learned that 65% of the human population – roughly four and one-half *billion* individuals – can unleash lethal force upon the innocent with little beyond mere prompting from an authority figures dressed in white lab coats.

Each one of us has seen instances of pedestrians bypassing wounded or dying individuals with *no apparent* desire to aid them. *Whom*, then, could you expect help from if you are suddenly confronted with an active shooter, homicide bomber, or deranged co-worker? The whole concept of there being an *Independent Counterterrorist* program was to provide you with your own, personal threat reduction operative – namely, *you yourself*.

Despite the popularity of the Second Edition, *more* has to be included. More intelligence collection has to be addressed. More tactical training methods have to be considered and developed. A more all-inclusive lifestyle and *system* has to be developed. As much as any *single* book can aspire to, this latest version of *Mini-Manual of the Independent Counterterrorist* will seek to push you into the proper direction. Because *no book* can solve life's problems for you, it will dispense with many of the trappings other books make available to you. That is, this neither is a how-to book nor is it an illustrated, coffee table edition. If you are seeking another [insert your favorite subject here] "bible", go read the *real thing*.

Being an "independent counterterrorist" means being isolated from *others* making decisions for you. Everyone else screwed the pooch; it is now time for you to step up to the plate and swing at real fastballs. Hopefully, this Third Edition will contain all the necessary information to get you to stand in the correct batter's box…

R.J. Godlewski
April 2014

# 1. STILL NEEDING TACTICAL CITIZENS

Have you ever seen a video or witnessed other people standing around and observing another individual being beaten, dying, or otherwise threatened without doing *something* about it? Do you know someone who goes catatonic as soon as adversity strikes? Have you ever met anyone who casts votes and yet remains clueless regarding politics, economics, and national security? Let us face it; the vast majority of the human population likely goes about his or her daily life with little thought beyond that which confronts their vision at that particular moment. Such people live solely for that week's paycheck, drive automobiles while talking on cell phones, and entrust teachers with the rearing of their children. None of them considers "What *if*?" To make matters far worse, scientists have proven that 65% of the human population can be induced into killing an innocent person with little more than "authoritative" prompting from another individual.[1] This means that *at least six of the next ten people that you encounter possess the inherent ability to kill* you with very little external motivation.

The "'Me' Generation" has silenced rational thought in education, politics, economics, religion, and life in general. Certainly within the four primal aspects that comprise fourth-generation warfare (4GW).[2] Big Brother has assured the world

---

[1] Dave Grossman, *On Killing: The Psychological Cost of Learning to Kill in War and Society* (New York: Back Bay Books, 2009), 142.
[2] Fourth-generation warfare (4GW), arguably a disputed term, signifies warfare simultaneously engaged within the martial, religious, political, and economic arenas.

that the masses – specifically representing your friends and neighbors – defer to the state without a moment's reflection upon whether 'the state' represents your best interests or not. We can see this within America by how many people equate the various "Occupy" crowds with goodness and the numerous Tea Party participants with abject evil despite overwhelming evidence to the contrary. Remember, anarchy flourishes with crowds, not one or two individuals. More dangerously, perhaps, rests the existence of the United Nations (UN), an organization that does very little but equalizes divergent countries. In fact, the UN could be considered, in modern socio-political terms, international affirmative action at best. Where the fault rests, unfortunately, is within any thought process that suggests that *actions* are equal.

Consider the UN in the light of domestic U.S. politics. Representative Nancy Pelosi (D-CA), over several years, reigned as Speaker of the House – the third in line to the U.S. Presidency. She was voted into office, however, by the district largely consisting of San Francisco, California. What this means, of course, is that the people of San Francisco placed into office a person whom the rest of the nation did not vote for or emphatically endorse, yet her decisions affected hundreds of millions. The UN represents the same problem; a myriad of smaller, largely insignificant nations could conspire to disrupt the planet over the objectives of those whose presence, experience, and talents have forged the opportunity for the UN to exist in the first place. This remains problematic, to say the least. At best, the UN indicts *all* international regulatory organizations – both good and bad.

The concept of a 'tactical citizen', without whom there could not be *independent* counterterrorists, rests upon the foundation that it remains *individuals* who hold personal responsibility for his or her actions. That is, there are good *people* as well as *bad* people, but *people* they remain. Neither automatons nor animals. *Every* individual person conceived on this planet bears the same inherent rights as *all other* individuals, irrespective of his or her place in life, race, nationality, religious beliefs, education, or physical beauty. What separates people from one another, therefore, remains exclusive to his or her personal actions and choices. The same holds true with groups of individuals, though responsibility for collective actions more often than not rests within the power of that particular group's leadership as group dynamics offers some measure of absolution.[3]

Because institutions – whether religions, organizations, governments, etc. – can be led astray by the actions of comparatively very few individuals (say, in the case of Nazi Germany), the holistic approach to social activities may be dangerous. The larger the organization, the greater the opportunity for the few to destroy the reputation and livelihood of the many. For example, consider how the actions of a relatively few individuals who abused prisoners at Abu Ghraib, gang-raped a 14-year-old girl in Mahmudiyah, Iraq, or killed innocent Afghan citizens in Maywand destroyed the reputation of the U.S. military and Americans in general.[4] That so few could destroy so many has been the hallmark of humanity ever since Cain took Abel out into the field to murder him.[5] Hence, the desperate need for *independence* (but never individualism) within the world and, more precisely, why *The Independent Counterterrorist* (ICT) represents neither an organization nor a doctrine.

The second edition of this book merged my *Tactical Citizen* and *The Independent Counterterrorist* programs[6] and

---

[3] Grossman, *On Killing*, 142.
[4] Clark C. Barrett, *Finding "The Right Way": Toward an Army Institutional Ethic* (Carlisle, PA: Strategic Studies Institute, September 2012), 2.
[5] The parable of Genesis 4:1-11 *New American Bible* remains that murder can arise from even the smallest (i.e., two) group. See the next chapter.
[6] Both programs emerged as a monthly, standalone training series with PDF documents posted on the Internet for ease and convenience. This book updates the previously release *Mini-Manual of The Independent Counterterrorist* and absorbs material from both efforts.

rested as a strict matter of convenience. The attributes of one who seeks to protect his or her family from threat and disaster (TC) remains as valid as one who personally seeks to stop domestic and transnational threats (ICT) against the broader community. Accordingly, some will likely feel more comfortable protecting his or her home whereas the more ambitious will likely seek to stop harm against the innocent. Nevertheless both are sorely needed in today's day and age as hostile groups – from various political, social, and religious affiliations – seek to disrupt others' "life, liberty, and the pursuit of happiness."

It remains an old adage that one picture is worth a thousand words. Unfortunately, many people are fascinated more with flashy photographs than learn to analyze events or writings. In this regard, you will find few photographs or diagrams within this book. It does not represent a training manual, *per se*. It remains intended as a reference guide to inspire *you* – the budding Independent Counterterrorist – to learn on your own. The greatest disadvantage in the world of battle remains to permit your adversary to understand what it is that you know. Therefore, to succeed within life, *do not* allow your enemies to know exactly what it is that you have learned and can do. Plant this seed, water it, nourish it, and permit it to grow to new heights.

### Concepts to Remember:

- *You* are responsible for your own safety and survival.
- *All* human beings warrant protection.
- Taxpayer-funded services remain an option, *not* an obligation.
- Threat resolution remains a *lifestyle* approach consisting of a great many decades of discipline.
- You will *always* have a great deal to learn.
- Think about tomorrow, but plan for *today's* challenges.
- Your greatest threat may be that which you have previously *ridiculed*.

# 2. THE IMPERATIVE TO FIGHT

Peace is the absence of hostility, the aberration of the human condition. Wars, however, have been around ever since Cain took out his brother Abel in a fit of religious jealousy. Whether you subscribe this to a Biblical story of historical accuracy or not, the moral remains that as long as there are at least *two* people around, conflict naturally arises and it may result within personal death or injury. If such conflict arises with only one person around; well, then, we have to come and take that person away for safekeeping.

You might also note that this first of recorded conflicts was, in fact, a *faith-induced* struggle. The Lord looked upon Abel's offering with favor but not upon Cain and his. This angered Cain immeasurably and the rest is history – people *are* different and their perceived blessings will inspire others into rage. Today, in the 21st century, the same situation occurs, developed over decades by shoddy post-Colonial politics. The Middle East and Northern Africa (MENA) remains a prime example where Israel has risen from abject poverty to build a democratic nation of posterity and success while Arabs, particularly those living within 'Palestine', descend into eternal poverty and grow envious of their Jewish neighbors. The Palestinians have simply descended into existence as perennial poster child of "the Cause" and few care to extract him or herself from the mess to forge a legitimate nation of his and her own. Blaming the West, and their avowed blood-right enemy Israel[7], appears easier to do than to fashion a

---

[7] Study the Biblical story of Ishmael and Isaac and how it relates to cultures where the first-born son receives full rights as heirs.

respectable life of one's own.

You would do well to begin a careful study of the rise of modern Israel with its conflicts among its neighbors, particularly its indefensible borders and significant 'illegal' immigration problem that represents something of a harbinger for difficulties associated with the United States' own national security. Israel's tactical problems today rest largely with this phantom nemesis of constantly shifting illegal immigrants.[8]

By the way, this is a good trait to nurture; to constantly read from within the historical narrative. Ours represents a world where the purveyors of mayhem remain a very well read bunch.[9] It would be to your distinct disadvantage to assume that Islamic and narco terrorists remain any less literate. What you need to add to this – which our Western leaders have failed to grasp – is that history exists to learn *from*; it does not represent an abstract archive of secretive documents that escape our attention. You, as a budding counterterrorist 'operative', possess ten thousand years of predecessors from which to learn and emulate. Our wars, though relatively modern and technologically superior to, say, the Peloponnesian War, are nevertheless as barbaric and 'one-on-one' as that great three-decade struggle between the Athenians and Spartans.

As it has been written, first off and straight away, *peace* represents the rarity amongst our kind. People, for whatever ill-conceived and instantaneous justification, will descend into conflict long before charitable pursuits are even acknowledged let alone pursued. If this were not the case, then we would come flying together with open arms and wallets whenever a natural catastrophe occurs. You will note that even here within

---

[8] Benny Morris, *Israel's Border Wars: 1949-1956* (New York: Oxford University Press, 1997), 118-184

[9] Paul Balor, *Manual of the Mercenary Soldier* (Boulder: Paladin Press, 1988), 22-23.

the compassionate United States, looting and sometimes even death occurs before the first telephone calls are made to relief agencies.

The *greatest* threat to your safety will come from that briefest hint of civility that descends upon you when the crisis hits the fan. You will, undoubtedly, think, "The authorities will restore order" or "I have lived here for decades and I have always managed to come through okay." There remains a first time for *everything*, do not forget. I have always characterized myself as "the most lethal individual that you will ever meet whose mannerisms and morality will betray his upbringing." In short, if I do not perceive you to be a threat to my existence, then neither do you need to perceive me to represent a threat to your safety. I do not segregate people through biases.

I have, on numerous occasions, physically defended myself against substantially larger opponents, sometimes even while in the presence of authority figures. I have employed whatever tool or weapon that I could lay my hands upon, be it pencil, hammer, or swinging meat hook. Therefore, there is little that I will not improvise upon in order to defend myself should the need arise at work or at home. Naturally, others sometimes exclaimed something to the effect of, "Did you not understand that you could have been fired?" I usually responded with, "Did you *not* understand that I could have been killed unless I defended my life?"

My line between brutality and civility exists, but it remains extremely sharp. I could go from one limit to the other in a literal heartbeat and so, too, must you if you truly want to survive within this crazy, mixed-up world of ours. Will our efforts *always* work? Who knows? All that we know is that we were born kicking and screaming for a chance at life and we have made it thus far. I will not accept an unnatural death without doing *something* to assure longevity. The rest remains up to God's Divine Providence and Will.

You have to present this mentality of eternal survival too. To go through life within a "daze" is not very conducive to this survival. Neither is remaining timid, which is what a great many of your neighbors prefer. Your terrorist enemies live for dying – rather, "martyrdom" – as long as they can kill as many of us Westerners as possible. It rests within their heritage, this Bedouin/Tribal form of Machiavellian reality. Some say do unto others before they do unto you. I say, that it remains all part of my fundamental rule governing combat: the victor determines what remains permissible or not.

It might seem to you, therefore, that to engage within battle against terrorists represents some form of blood ritual – and you are most emphatically correct in this belief. It *is* a blood ritual with catastrophic implications. Fighting terrorism represents, always remember, basic human *survival* at its most subconscious level. Even the horribly brutal battles of the 'World Wars' of the past century followed mathematical theory with astonishing accuracy.[10] Terrorism and guerrilla warfare, by their nature, are less formularized though I, for one, could easily adapt the 1920s Italian study of predator-prey models worked out to understand the rise in Mediterranean sharks during World War I to today's terrorist groups.[11] They representing the sharks and innocent civilians representing the prey. However, let us leave differential equations to the academics and syndicated television heroes.

Armies may be somewhat predictable, but humans are not nearly so and with the onslaught unleashed upon al-Qaeda since the September 11, 2001 attacks in New York City and Washington, jihadist groups have "franchised" into ever smaller, decentralized, and unpredictable social units. What this means for you, is that you will more than likely be

---

[10] Martin Braun, *Differential Equations and Their Applications* (New York: Springer-Verlag, 1993), 405.
[11] Ibid., 443-451.

encountering *individuals* – people who will think, function, and respond in a manner not fully isolated from your own. Or, according to accepted Darwinian Law: "The more similar two species are, the fiercer is the struggle for existence between them."[12] This fact explains a great deal about the modern Arab-Israeli conflict, but do not worry about perceived commonalities. You will have your own razor sharp dividing line to keep your own brutality one toe into reality.

Regardless of personal inhibitions, there *is* historical precedence for your emulating the terrorists in intensity, if not in tactics or beliefs. The United States won the Plains Indian Wars of 1865 to 1879 by going head-to-head with the American Indians instead of cozying up to them diplomatically. As General Nelson A. Miles said, "They have been petted and, if that policy is continued, they will furnish warriors for the next twenty years."[13] General Miles knew of what he spoke and his words resonate today as many politicians and leading citizens attempt to accord *our* Constitutional rights to foreign enemies captured and tried upon foreign soil. Miles's thoughts of the situation then – of treating hostiles "more as conquerors than prisoners"[14] – resonates today in court actions over Guantanamo Bay detainees such as 9/11 mastermind, Khalid Sheik Muhammad and his kind.

Understand, I am *not* denying the role of hate here in order to make it more palatable to vanquish our enemies.[15] Nor am I denying my own role in *dehumanizing* these thugs for the same result.[16] I merely offer that hate simply represents another side of the coin upon which love rests and I love

---

[12] Ibid., *bc.*
[13] Robert L. Utley, "Crook and Miles: Fighting and Feuding on the Indian Frontier," *MHQ: The Quarterly Journal of Military History* (Autumn 1989): 89.
[14] Ibid.
[15] Dave Grossman, *On Killing: The Psychological Cost of Learning to Kill in War and Society* (New York: Back Bay Books, 2009), 80-81.
[16] Ibid., 161.

America so much that I absolutely *hate anyone* messing with her or targeting her citizens. *Period.* End of discussion. Therefore, I hold no qualms, say, of taking out terrorists before they have a chance to plot, plan, or prepare for our extinction. As the *Catechism of the Catholic Church* so eloquently states:

> *"Nor is it necessary for salvation that a man omit the act of moderate self-defense to avoid killing the other man, since one is bound to take more care of one's own life than of another's."*[17]

"Moderate self-defense" to me represents a double-tap to the Jihadist's head and I, personally, see little problem in facing my Maker on the subject. My argument would be, "If he had not lifted a finger to harm me, then he would *still* be alive today." I will gladly face the fires of eternal damnation for something that *I did* but I will be damned if I am going to fry for what others forced me to do.

Listen, people, our lives are *not* ours, our nation is *not* ours, and our freedoms certainly are *not* ours *if we allow someone to take them away from us unopposed*. Everything within our society – from our tornado sirens to our police and fire departments and on up through the Department of Homeland Security – is based upon the concept of *reaction*. We need to plan for proactive *response*. If we allow our lives to be governed according to outside influence, whether waiting for the sirens to tell us to seek cover from an approaching twister or having the federal government instruct us on which nations are safe to visit, then we must accept that at *some point* in the future, that influence will become inadequate for *our particular situation*.

I would propose that a fundamental reason that you are reading this book is one of simple curiosity (probably *not* as

---

[17] United States Catholic Conference, Inc. *Catechism of the Catholic Church* (New York: Doubleday, 1994), Paragraph #2264.

curious as if you were reading *Skills of the Assassin*). That is good, for curiosity helps keep you alive. Just remember that curiosity eventually killed the cat in the fable. What you need to be is *prepared* and so; if you find yourself reading these words, let it become a way of life for you, this obsession with survival. Do not let a moment go by without first and foremost thinking of how you can come back home safely at the end of the day. Chances are, for the most part, that you have become too accustomed to relying solely upon, well, *chance*. Not anymore, friend.

I want you to be reading this book because you understand the primal nature of the threat; that we cannot always rely upon our brave men and women in the military or federal government to protect us *one hundred percent* of the time. And your friends and neighbors, if not most of your family, will be hopelessly inadequate to come to your aid during any form of crisis situation.

Before we proceed, I want you to make a promise to *yourself* – not to me, your wife, or Auntie Busty. I want you to promise yourself that you will begin every day of every week of every year reminding yourself of the following words:

> "*The ruling to kill the Americans and their allies – civilian and military – is an individual duty for every Muslim who can do it in any country in which it is possible to do it..*"

**Sheikh Usamah Bin-Muhammed Bin-Laden and Ayman al-Zawahiri, February 23, 1998.**

Bin Laden may be dead – thank God – but Zawahiri and hundreds of thousands of their supporters are not, and nearly every one of them has read this *published* decree. Print these words, as well as the following released by Bin Laden's official spokesman nine months after the 9/11/2001 attacks upon a series of Post-It Notes® and place them where you will be able to read them:

> *"We have the right to kill 4 million Americans – 2 million of them children – and to exile twice as many and wound and cripple hundreds of thousands."*

**Suleiman Abu Gheith.** [18]

Bin Laden may indeed be dead, but the threat from al-Qaeda has only begun. What confronts us today represents a kaleidoscope of lone wolves and covert cells resembling the 2009 Fort Hood massacre suspect, the ill-fated Christmas Day bomber, and the vile murderers of our ambassador in Benghazi during September 11, 2012. Do *not* believe our politicians when they say that the threat has either been diminished because of Bin Laden's death (the Pakistanis have been making noise saying that he was ill and out of the picture anyway and Bin Laden certainly watched enough pornography at his Abbottobad home to suggest this as plausible), or that al-Qaeda is on the run.

### Concepts to Remember:
- People fight, surrender, or die.
- *You* are the *only* person who will go everywhere and do everything with you.
- Surviving means having to do some things you do not want to do.
- Nature provides you with tools and weapons for defense, but only humans can consciously employ them or not.
- Despite how you feel about the world, a large percentage of it *already* wants you dead for no reason acceptable to logic.
- Murder remains a grave crime. Killing is *not.*
- There remains no shame in exercising either self-preservation and/or self-promotion.

---

[18] Graham Allison, *Nuclear Terrorism: The Ultimate Preventable Catastrophe* (New York: Times Books, 2004), 12.

## 3. THE ROLE OF RELIGION IN SURVIVAL

For most Christian Americans, prayer represents a deeply private affair, even amongst your more vocal fundamentalists who seek to better the world largely through the context of the secular state.[19] For Islamists, however, spiritual life and daily, public life remains inseparable.[20] We, in the West, appear to have outgrown our reliance upon all things "religious" for our daily needs. We have lost this intimate companionship with the divine that existed for nearly 1,300 years until we began to fabricate other "faiths" to fill the void.[21] This de-Christianization of our culture, perhaps more prominent in Great Britain and Europe, has set us up for savage attacks by those who have chosen to more consciously embrace their religious militancy.[22]

Listen to what real, *documented* faith can lead one to do, in this case involving mystic St. Simeon Stylites (390? – 459 A.D.) of Syria:

> "Simeon built himself a column six feet high and lived on it. Ashamed of his moderation, he built and lived on ever taller columns, until he made his permanent abode on a pillar sixty feet high. Its circumference at the top was little more than three feet; a railing kept the saint from falling to

---

[19] Fawaz A. Gerges, *Journey of the Jihadist: Inside Muslim Militancy* (Orlando: Harcourt, 2006), 35.
[20] Ibid.
[21] Peter Kreeft, *Everything that you ever wanted to know about Heaven…but never dreamed of asking* (San Francisco: Ignatius Press, 1990), 193.
[22] Ibid.

the ground in his sleep. On this perch Simeon lived uninterruptedly for thirty years, exposed to rain and sun and cold. A ladder enabled disciples to take him food and remove his waste. He bound himself to the pillar by a rope; the rope became embedded in his flesh, which putrefied around it, stank, and teemed with worms; Simeon picked up the worms that fell from his sores, and replaced them there, saying to them, 'Eat what God has given you.'"[23]

Imagine hoisting your office chair upon a sixty-foot high flagpole and then residing there "uninterruptedly" for *thirty years.*

Since few records ever remain unbroken, Simeon's followers – and there were many, known simply as the Stylites – matched his feat for periods of up to *sixty* years in duration. And you cannot sit through your boss's Monday morning lecture without thinking about the coffee pot. Is it any wonder, then, how badly we have lost touch with our own cultural heritage? Could any of the great cathedrals in Europe, many constructed over the course of *centuries*, ever be built within technologically advanced but hopelessly secularized today? So-called "Separation of Church and State" individuals who, more often than not, make up a decided minority of the population immediately slap any community that places even a plaque of the Ten Commandments anywhere in public with a lawsuit. What would the ACLU do with a *four-hundred year* public works project to build a single church?

What we are faced with, in our battle against modern Islamic extremists (and quite possibly a significant portion of

---

[23] Will Durant, *The Age of Faith* (New York: Simon and Schuster, 1950), 60.

the overall Muslim population[24]), remains a foe that possesses the gut determination and patience of a Saint Simeon Stylites with the diabolical hatred of an Osama Bin Laden or an Ayman al-Zawahiri. In other words, people who can remain isolated for thirty years and still shout out to the world "Kill Americans! Military *and* civilian! Kill *two million American children!*"

How does the West respond? We blame subsequent attacks, such as that which killed American Ambassador to Libya, Chris Stevens, and three others in Benghazi on September 11, 2012 as spontaneous demonstrations protesting some obscure YouTube video clip that no one heretofore realized existed. My then 85-year-old mother understood that the attack upon our consulate as well as the attack against our Embassy in Cairo represented a terrorist attack. Apparently, our government did not.

When waging psychological warfare against our opponents – a fundamental element of the war against terrorism – we need to spread *our* message passionately, indulging within color, symbolism, folklore, and the pure emotion of the religiously tuned human spirit.[25] Historically, the individuals of the world have been challenged by conflicting arguments of *"'It's a horrible idea for you to change your ways...'* and *'Brother, have I got something great in store for you!'"*[26] In this context, it serves no one to try to win 'hearts and minds' without the stomach to back one's pledges up with.

Nevertheless, we tread upon a very slippery slope whenever we rely solely upon religious faith to guide us

---

[24] Many experts believe that radicalized Muslims account for "only" 10-20% of the global Muslim population. Taken at 15%, the figure exceeds the estimates of the total number of combatants during 1939-1945 of ~105,542,100 individuals. Source: John Ellis, *World War II: The Encyclopedia of Facts and Figures* (Military Book Club, 1993), 253-254.

[25] Balor, *Mercenary Soldier*, 217.

[26] R.J. Godlewski, "Latte Intelligence: The Divorce of Shock Creativity and Special Information Operations" *American Intelligence Journal* 29 no. 1 (2011): 72.

through the chaotic events enveloping the battlefield.[27] Many a 16th century individual believed that God alone would deflect cannonballs and had to turn and flee in horror when projectile physics overpowered prayer on the fields of North-Central Europe.[28] If only we could be as sterilizing in our routing out of ideological fanatics today.

The only role that religious faith should – and *needs* to – serve today remains strictly within the motivational sector. We *need* to be highly motivated, primarily we "average" citizens, or else our more 'inspired' enemies will gladly blow themselves apart in our midst while our minds are preoccupied with sports, Hollywood, food, and a myriad of other distractions. There is, after all, nothing inherently wrong with shouting out, "Hot damn! Praise the Lord! Did you see the tight grouping that I placed between the bastard's eyes?" whenever we are calming down *after an attack by a dozen armed assailants* (assuming there are no cops or lawyers present to recall our statement). It is when we resort to "Please, dear Lord. Kindly deflect those Katyusha rockets away from me" while we are standing out in the open that things get to be a little dicey.

God does not play favorites with free will. He might tweak the human psyche every now and then or disrupt the natural world for a brief moment, but He does not manhandle the situation. Even Christ acknowledged that people *could* do harm to Him if God the Father permitted it to happen.[29] He knew that when crisis and aggravation bore their ugly heads, there would not be another living soul around prepared to die to save an innocent life – *even* His. Times have *not* changed any today.

---

[27] Billy Waugh and Tim Keown, *Hunting the Jackal: A Special Forces and CIA Soldier's Fifty Years on the Frontlines of the War Against Terrorism* (New York: Avon Books, 2004), 145.
[28] Ralph Peters, "Rebels and Religion: How Fighters become Fanatics," *Armed Forces Journal* (January 2007): 31.
[29] John 19:11, *NAB*.

Enemies, you understand, make for strange bedfellows. Common foes unite common enemies. Shia and Sunni Muslims band together to wage war against the West. Sailors and Marines become good friends during the Army-Navy game. Communist China and Islamic jihadists emerge as kindred spirits in the pursuit of opportunity.[30] And progressive liberals join with the Islamists to spoil Christianity around the planet. God, for His divine role, resembles a hovering classroom instructor. He would *like* to nudge us into the correct direction, perhaps even "sneeze" out the answer, but God knows that the *only* sure way that we *will learn* is by solving the problem *ourselves*. This is how we learn to forgive by accepting the bad things that (occasionally) happen.

Thus for every evil person on the planet that does something terribly wrong, God provides us with thousands upon thousands of individuals that should, conceivably, fill the "Good Samaritan" role. It remains for *us* to find a way to use those particular talents, interests, and needs that He has bestowed upon us to survive within this maddening world of ours. That, friend, is where *you* come into the picture.

You understand that Islamic jihadists want to destroy as many of us as they can. You know that they want to establish a universal caliphate that extends beyond the boundaries that existed in 750 A.D. You see it within their actions – and within their intent – everyday on the television news and Internet. Their actions speak louder than words, even louder than the homicide bombings that destroy weddings, crowded shopping malls, and the gunfire that rips through military command centers and recruiting posts. You realize that from *your perspective*, the only good terrorist is a dead one. At least an apprehended and *well-incarcerated* one.

What you might not understand, however, is that if *you*

---

[30] H. John Poole, *Dragon Days: Time for "Unconventional" Tactics* (Emerald Isle, NC: Posterity Press, 2007), 3-23.

– the concerned citizen with the seven children throwing food at one another during the evening meal – do not do *something* to stem the tide, then nobody else may. There remains a reason, friend, that you are lucky enough to have that nice comfortable home with the seven brats driving your wife insane. For, perhaps, the whole of your life you have been accustomed to placing complete faith in *your* military, *your* federal agencies, and *your* local police departments to protect *your* extremities should the need arise.

Guess what? Economic evolution dictates that as the world grows more populous and competitive, those forces provided by taxpayers will diminish in both size and effectiveness. They are *not yours*; they respond for a community of which you just happen to belong. As terrorists, drug traffickers, and other transnational criminal elements inch ever closer to possessing "death rays" and other weapons of mass destruction, our local and national politicians will continue to dawdle over, say, passing laws acknowledging our *natural right* to own and bear firearms for self-defense.

Politicians, simply by virtue of their trade, represent cowards. It remains the truth. They will bend over backwards to accommodate those they fear but will sacrifice those they actually represent. If you cannot trust that another individual would come to your aid when the need arises, then you certainly *cannot* trust that a politician will see to *your* needs beforehand. This, friend, is where being "religious" definitely comes in handy.

To engage personal survival alone and, frankly, at great odds requires one to be highly motivated and possess self-confidence that is to be considered rather remarkable within today's day and age. You must not only *anticipate* survival within a wide variety of situations, you must actually *believe* it. This is not very easy, especially when surviving within today's environment requires you to be on your toes one hundred percent of the time. For instance, I preach remaining within your 360° sphere of personal awareness as imperative. That said, I understand that after, say, walking eight to ten miles in the sun or other adverse conditions, a person's senses dull. It is just natural.

Therefore, if you cannot present "superhuman capabilities", it helps to be able to call upon superhuman *beliefs*. In other words, religious beliefs *can* provide you with that added spunk or incentive that you need to remain alert when you are getting tired from twenty-mile marches or being shot at. Past martyrs and saints came from little different backgrounds than you probably do, but what made them *special* was how they used their individual faith to bear them through extraordinarily horrendous events. St. Sebastian was pierced repeatedly by arrows unleashed from Mauritanian archers, briefly healed, and then eventually had to be clubbed to death. In 17th century Japan, British Captain Richard Cocks saw Christian children as young as five and six years old burned alive within their mother's arms. Later, in about 1650 A.D., the total number of Christians killed in Japan approximated 200,000 to 300,000 individuals. During the Second World War, Saint Maxmillian Kolbe offered his own life in exchange for a married man with children who was about to be executed within a Nazi concentration camp.

Each one of us believes in *something* greater than him or her. It might be God, the United States Constitution, or simply "Life, liberty, and the pursuit of happiness." Regardless, it defines what makes us work hard, protect our families, and keep physically and mentally fit. People with a sound purpose rarely represent pathetic souls. Normally. If you consciously choose to go to war against terrorists – an assumption made by your reading these words – then you *must devote your entire life to the endeavor*. Slack for a moment, and the Beast will devour you. Say what you want, but *religious faith* provides you with an added edge; the personal power and integrity that will keep you motivated to "crush, kill, destroy" along with the sanctity to do so *only* to protect innocent human lives.

There remains a model of human behavior that equates our species with that of canines. In this manner, there exists wolves (sociopaths), packs of wild dogs (gangs and aggressive armies), sheep dogs (soldiers, police officers, and proactive citizens), and, of course, sheep (everyone else).[31] You have to make a personal and lasting decision on which group that you wish to run with; which "animal" best identifies your truest intent. As for myself, I am proud to aspire with the sheepdogs – I remain friendly, lovable, and loyal, but when aroused I can sink my fangs into even the most vicious wolf in order to protect my clan. My religious faith provides me with this sense of immortal duty. My Polish temper helps too.

Sadly, not everyone inhabiting our planet shares this belief. At best, they feel that religion represents an enemy, not a tool to empower the human spirit. At worst, they use *their* religious beliefs to segregate individuals and destroy "infidel" nations. God, for the former group, represents an affront to the human intellect. For the latter, He represents a military commander guiding the righteous towards global domination. Both parties are inherently wrong. God exists for *all* human individuals, even those who consciously choose to deny, ignore or hide from Him.

Both groups, unfortunately, feel that *Christianity* remains the only religious faith unacceptable to the human population. Radicalized Islam appears tolerated by secularists. Remember, however, this remains because secularists often ally themselves with the Islamists and arm your own intentions accordingly. From this point forward, you are either going to be associated with them or you are going to establish yourself as a threat to their agenda. Are you *ready*? Good.

---

[31] David A. Grossman, "Defeating the Enemy's Will: The Psychological Foundations of Maneuver Warfare" in *Maneuver Warfare: An Anthology*, ed. Richard D. Hooker, Jr. (Novato, CA: Presidio Press, 1993), 175.

Take a brief moment and walk over to the nearest mirror. Gaze into the reflection deeply and analyze yourself thoughtfully. How well does the visual image mesh with the spiritual character of which we have just discussed? This is not a silly test; *anyone* venturing into the world of private, independent counterterrorism operations must be able to judge two-dimensional representations of three-dimensional figures (as befitting photographs and videos). Unfortunately, most people are far too critical – "I am too fat", "my hair looks ridiculous", "when did *that* grow?" – but profound analysis is still intimately possible. What do *you* see staring back at you?

Reflections in mirrors simply represent visual templates fitted over emotional thoughts. Our eyes blink when we are nervous, our complexion lightens when we are ill, and even our skin vibrates whenever we are anxious. These things *can* be seen by the observant eye and they bear upon our spiritual foundation. It has been said that holy people are happy and superficial ones are sad. Which one are you?

Do you possess the supernatural beliefs necessary to carry you through the day? It shows within the reflection (please do not employ cameras to do this; most lenses are accurate enough to convince any adult that they are on the verge of fracturing away). One of my favorite scenes in a movie is when the centurion is just about to whip Jesus for providing Ben-Hur (Charlton Heston in the 1959 movie of the same name) with a drink of water against the soldier's orders. The audience simply sees the back of Jesus as he stands up to confront the soldier. What is not hidden from view, however, remains the look upon the Roman's face and his "confused" response to the disobedience that Jesus had committed.

One can only imagine the "look" that the real Jesus would have delivered to the soldier. Some individuals can break the largest of bullies with a momentary glance (just ask some wives!), if they but possess sufficient confidence in themselves. Where, in the mirror, does *your* confidence reign?

Are you capable of starring down (albeit extremely briefly, it is hoped) a terrorist? A drug trafficker? A garden-variety criminal? What does your mirror suggest? Probably not much, at least at the present. That is okay, however, because your first impression may have a lot to do with your physical conditioning. *Everyone* – including your Tier 1 Navy SEAL and Army Delta Force types can improve a little. Where you benefit is that you will *not* have to condition yourself the way they do.

### Concepts to Remember:

- Religion represents the basis for human life, certainly the spirit of human history.
- Even hardcore atheists remain influenced by religious faith.
- Religion is most emphatically a social issue – contrasting with *faith*, which represents a personal belief.
- The primary threat against any religion is *politics*.
- In the West, *religion* remains subjective.
- Religion represents the most powerful weapon within any army's arsenal.
- Religion, as an obstacle or fortress, cannot be defeated.
- Ridiculing religion merely serves to magnify its potential.

# 4. CONDITIONING THE WARRIOR YOU

Now that you have decided to take a stand against the terrorists and transnational criminal elements hell-bent on your personal destruction, again, it behooves you to take stock of your physical and mental condition. Chances are you are in far worse shape than you care to admit. Not all is lost, fortunately, for the tools that you need to recover the fitness of your youth remain all around you. First, however, we need to work on your mental attitude.

## A Warrior's Mind

When confronted with danger, a person has but four distinct options available.[32]

- **Fight.** A person can stand his or her ground and fight the crisis at hand;
- **Posture.** A person can stand his or her ground, but instead of fighting will 'flair up' and present a more threatening image in the hope that their adversary will capitulate or flee;
- **Flight.** An individual can give ground and make a hasty retreat back towards safety;
- **Submit.** An individual can simply give up and surrender, accepting whatever conditions the victor may place upon them.

---

[32] Grossman, *On Killing*, 7.

To surrender or run takes very little initiative and therefore I will not discuss these two options. The other two – and quite probably, various combinations of them – represent what needs discussion when dealing with terrorists and other criminal elements. Posturing exists as, perhaps, the more active of the two and therefore we shall begin our discussion with it.

Posturing simply represents inflating one's image to compensate for or hide one's physical inabilities. This is what happens when your neighbor's pet Chihuahua begins barking like a Rottweiler whenever you approach their "territory" too closely. You realize that you can stomp the little bugger into the ground without effort, but the dog believes that maybe, just *maybe*, if they act mean and vicious enough, you just might go off into another direction. Humans are not generally so accommodating; therefore, we have to fabricate artificial methods of making ourselves look scary when confronted by our own kind.

Whether the disciplined approach of a Greek phalanx, the ridiculously inappropriate hats of the Napoleonic era, or the terrifying 'rebel yell' of the Southern Confederacy, people try their best to make themselves *appear* threatening to their enemies in the hope that they will either flee or capitulate.[33] During the Second World War, Germans placed sirens on their Stuka dive-bombers to terrify targeted populations, a tactic recorded for posterity within various newsreels from the conflict.

Examples that are more recent flow from your favorite sports team. Whether from their sideline antics or insistence upon slapping gruesome graffiti all over their arms in the form of tattoos, they try to get the entire planet to know that they remain big, bad athletes who intend to vanquish their

---

[33] Grossman, "Defeating the Enemy's Will," 155.

opponents. Generally, however, they do not. Those that eventually do win largely represent the non-descript players who have actually *prepared* for the challenge.

Posturing may work for you but I recommend against it unless needed, for instance, to cover an escape and evasion effort should you ever find yourself deep behind "enemy lines" even if that merely represents the inner cities of Detroit, New York, Los Angeles, etc. In our case, as an independent counterterrorist operative, posturing may call *unwanted attention* to your efforts and, without proper backup; you will unnecessarily place yourself and your loved ones in jeopardy. More important for you, obviously, remains the motivation to fight and survive.

Like-species rarely ever turn upon one another for the kill, acquiescing to the primal law designed to prevent extinction. Elk will lock antlers and battle one another for hours until one side capitulates, but these same elk will immediately use their racks to devastating effect upon a wolf or a coyote. Humans, on the other hand, largely have to devise unnatural methods in which to kill one another. We possess our mathematical formulae and our scientific equations.[34] However, it has been admirably stated that the scientific study of men in combat is like "a world of virgins studying sex, with nothing to go on but porno films."[35] For our purposes, we shall only discuss one particular scientific study that relates to our personal conditioning.

During the 1960s, Dr. Stanley Milgram of Yale University conducted a study involving human obedience and aggressive behavior and discovered that *over sixty-five percent* (65%) of the human population could be readily manipulated into delivering a "lethal" charge of electricity upon a total stranger.[36] Moreover, these test subjects continued to

---

[34] Braun, *Differential Equations*, 398-414.
[35] Grossman, "Defeating the Enemy's Will," 144.
[36] Ibid.

inflict this torture – even *increasing the voltage* – until long after the victims would have really been dead.[37] This research has since been validated by subsequent studies within dozens of countries.[38]

What allows people to commit such acts? How can normal, everyday subjects be induced into inflicting such pain upon the innocent? There exist several methods:[39]

- If the person is within proximity to an authority figure, they may be inclined to obey for fear of ridicule or punishment. Conversely, they may be inclined to perform as expected out of fear that should they fail, their leader may be replaced with someone far worse;

- If the person is a member of a group, they will perform more effectively for fear of being labeled as the "weakest link". Being within any group also provides the individual with a sense of conformity and accountability;

- Through modern technology, individuals can establish a *physical distance* between themselves and their victims. Nobody thinks twice about seeing images of a B-52 dropping its load over a mountain target, for example, but when that same individual sees images of brutal, hand-to-hand fighting within a major city, they more fully understand the true devastation of war. The further they remain from their target – through the use of hand grenades to rifles on through artillery and long-range aircraft – their resistance towards killing dissolves proportionately;

- Individuals can also increase the *emotional distance*

---

[37] Ibid.
[38] Ibid.
[39] Grossman, *On Killing*, 187-194.

between them and their victim, employing hate (such as that targeted towards specific ethnic, religious, or racial differences, etc.) to *dehumanize* victims, thus making it far easier to kill them. This is the technique employed to get gullible young Muslims to murder "infidels" en masse; the combination of Westerners representing non-Muslim individuals and the tempting reward of paradise persuades them to commit the unthinkable. Individuals can also increase the emotional separation from their victims by shielding their faces or shooting them in the back of the head where the victim's eyes do not suggest humanity and require concern.

You, in your independent efforts to combat terrorism, will be lacking in both proximity to any authoritative figure as well as the benefits of group camaraderie. This is one reason why we discussed religion previously; a religious element within your life can – and should – provide you with a sense of both. Religion – of whatever personal choice – can provide you with an authority figure to follow and be afraid of angering. It can also provide you with an established doctrine followed by millions of believers around the world. In decidedly Christian America, the choice of adherence remains easy.[40]

Christianity remains part of our American heritage, our communities, and undoubtedly part of our families. Our founding fathers not only invoked God in nearly every document they produced, they used Christian doctrine in formulating our path towards independence. We may not wish to reflect upon this and God knows that in our ultra-politically correct world, religion remains very much taboo – *specifically*

---

[40] The U.S. Central Intelligence Agency (CIA) places the Christian population at ~ 76.8%. See https://www.cia.gov/library/publications/the-world-factbook/geos/us.html. Accessed October, 2012. Adherents.com places this figure at ~ 82%. See http://www.adherents.com/rel_USA.html. Accessed October, 2012.

Christianity – but facts remain facts. George Washington, our very first president, declared it quite "impossible to rightly govern a nation without God and the Bible". If only Washington the city were as devout as Washington the man was.

I suspect, however, that you are reading these words because you do not care very much about what others may think of you. You understand that Islamic jihadists have targeted Americans and other Westerners for death. You know that drug traffickers remain on the verge of destroying Mexico and, perhaps, sending millions of "narco-refugees" fleeing north for the semblance of security within the United States.[41] You understand that these various groups will *not* stop until they *are* stopped and that you realize that military and federal resources remain finite in scope. Thus, you have decided that *you* must become a solution to the problem and want to do *something* to protect yourself and your loved ones from these vile thugs masquerading as legitimate human beings. Well, compadre, chances are that you are doing so from a *religious* perspective.

If you desire to take a stand against Islamic, narco, and political terrorism, I am willing to bet that you are doing so because of one or more of the following reasons:

- You do not want anyone enforcing their beliefs upon you;

- You do not subscribe to the beliefs that others are trying to force upon you;

- You believe that *all people were created equal* and are possessing of certain inalienable rights;

---

[41] Paul Rexton Kan, *Mexico's "Narco-Refugees": The Looming Challenge for U.S. National Security* (Carlisle, PA: Strategic Studies Institute, October 2011), 25-29.

- You detest the use of indiscriminate violence against innocents as a means of affecting political change;

- You believe within established law and order as determined by duly elected and/or appointed officials as determined by the citizenry;

- You value your life above all others, with the possible exception of your spouse and immediate family;

- You believe that it remains individuals and families, *not* governments or political leaders, which form the foundation of society.

Whether you care to admit it or not, *all* of these came to be as the result of religious beliefs – specifically Western Judeo-Christian beliefs. Furthermore, religion can provide the independent operative a sense of companionship to fall back upon during trying times. Again, knowing that millions of Christian martyrs had suffered through often worse things before may aid you in understanding the inherent power within your own faith while you are being targeted by, say, fanatical Islamists. Also, remaining in communion with an established set of beliefs – for example, the 2,000+ year tradition of the Roman Catholic Mass has remained virtually unaltered since before Saint Justin explained the proceedings to pagan emperor Antoninus Pius around the year 155 A.D.[42] – provides you with an infinitely larger group of people who may support your efforts.

Knowing that you represent, in the case of Christianity, only one of over a billion and a half "non-Islamists", will help you corral the most powerful tool ever invented for waging war – *raw hatred.* Ironically, this represents our downfall in Western, Christian culture – we allow ourselves to be

---

[42] *Catechism*, #1345.

repeatedly attacked because we just cannot understand how "some" people can actually hate one another to do the sort of things that terrorists and other criminals do. Let us leave that to psychologists, sociologists, and theologians to debate. For you, however, just be thankful that humans *can* hate.

I consider myself just as loving and as compassionate as the next person. I want to defeat cancer, build schools in Asia, provide healthcare to Africa, and spread economic development in Eastern Europe. Still, like the loyal and devoted sheepdog, I can become extremely vicious when my "flock" is threatened. That is, I absolutely *hate* tyrants, terrorists, and transnational criminals. I do not particularly care what religion they practice, what system of belief they endorse, or even what nationality or ethnic group they come from.

If you threaten me or mine, I will hurt you *severely* or die in the process of trying. I will use a combat knife to rip your throat out, an elephant gun to tear your head off, or a "death ray" to send your clan back into the Stone Age never to be found by any future anthropologist. How can I make such claims? Because I absolutely, positively *hate* people who prey upon unsuspecting innocents. Yes, we all remain a little devious or perhaps disingenuous, but I am not talking about the neighbor who forgets to return your garden shears or the kid that breaks into the house across the street to steal Playboy® magazines for his older brother (guilty as charged, I might add).

When it comes to terrorists, I for one do not classify them as *human* and I am not afraid to admit as much. What kind of father plans his death in a homicide bombing to kill non-aggressive soldiers and what kind of mother permits their four-year-old son to watch continuously the videotape of the child's father killing himself and others?[43] That child is unlikely to grow up to become anything but another homicide bomber with a complete disregard for innocent human life. It is because I personally consider "human" to represent a form of office that I can make such distinctions. For instance, a spirit may be either an angel or a demon depending upon their specific nature and the office they may or may not hold. In this regard, not all *Homo sapiens* should be considered as *human*. Personal beliefs aside, I do not waste time equating an Osama Bin Laden or an Ayman al-Zawahiri with either Mother Theresa or the Dalai Lama. Yes, each professed a certain religious belief and, yes, each represented a member of the *H. sapiens* species. The difference remains that I would gladly donate to Mother Theresa's surviving organization or tip my hat to the Dalai Lama and his followers, but would just *love* to see al-Qaeda and related Islamist groups nuked into non-existence.

What you, the budding independent counterterrorist, must *not* do, however, is become all consumed by hate alone. You must ensure that the flipside of the emotion – *love* – remains fully extended to your fellow man. Do not profess killing terrorists for the sake of killing fellow *people*. Strive to protect the *innocent* instead. The terrorists *are* consumed by raw hatred. They *do* want to kill for the sake of killing. You are much better than that.

You desire to *serve* life, even if just your own. They want life to serve *them*, and there is a distinction just as there is a distinction between your viciousness and theirs. Remember, we are talking about sheepdogs and wolves here. One attack unprovoked; the other merely defends. When left alone, there remains little to differentiate the sheepdog from their attendant flock.

---

[43] Hala Jaber, *Hezbollah: Born With a Vengeance* (New York: Colombia University Press, 1997), 1.

You may also note that there is usually a *single* sheepdog attending that flock, not an "army" of dogs or battalions. Just one. It may even surprise you that, historically, it has been *private enterprise* that first offered protection against terrorists and that taxpayer-funded "official" forces developed *from* them.[44] Regardless, individuals "have a perfect right to protect themselves, or to hire people to protect them and their property."[45] It has always been that way in the United States, so you are not doing anything particularly new here.

What makes you a breath of fresh air is that the vast majority of your neighbors have opted out for remaining *sheep*. We – you and I and our compatriots – are tired of having wool pulled over our eyes. We see the Islamists targeting America. We see the Muslim *ummah* shamefully silent on the issue. We see the narcotics traffickers continually disregarding our borders and our sovereignty. We see the political leadership in Washington, too, shamefully silent on the issue. We understand that *something must be done* to protect our lives even if it means actually going to war against the terrorists *ourselves*.

### A Warrior's Body

Now that your mind is beginning to see through the clutter of inept political bodies and apathetic communities, it is time to get your body conditioned. No need to fear, however, as even nice middle-class kids have emerged from self-imposed training regimens with the capacity to slit throats with great efficiency.[46] Of course, *that* might be just a wee bit too drastic for you – until someone tries to murder your son or rape your teenage daughter. Then, by all means, rip their

---

[44] Christopher Dobson and Ronald Payne, *Counterattack: The West's Battle Against the Terrorists* (New York: Facts on File, 1982), 163.
[45] Ibid., 164.

innards to shreds. It remains up to you.

Nevertheless, it is *not* my intention within this book to teach you to kill – or even *tell* you to kill. That is not what I am all about here. Only *you* can decide what needs to be done during any particular moment or crisis. Already, far too many people are out there providing you with conflicting suggestions and recommendations beyond what needs discussion. First, however, you will probably have your hands full simply whipping your body back into tolerable shape.

To begin with, there is only *one* thing that is keeping you from having a body in good shape: excuses. Similarly, there is only one thing that is keeping you from possessing a body in *great* shape: lack of discipline. For starters, let us work towards the first step in getting you on your way to leading commando raids against hardened terrorist targets – getting you off your sofa and away from the television. Inactivity can add *twenty* pounds to even the most conscientious individual. I know, because this represents the exact amount that I gained when I ceased walking four miles each way to town (and when on Sundays, wearing a suit and tie with dress boots no less) and returned to full-time university studies.

You can still partake of cheeseburgers, pizza, brownies, cheesecake, etc. and just about anything else that you wish to devour. The point is, however, to take things in *moderation*. No need to "Super Size" everything. I, for instance, may eat two cheeseburgers for evening meal, but might skip lunch or eat something simple such as a banana. Chicken stir-fries are good; especially since you can load the meal with peppers and other vegetable ingredients (I personally add sautéed mushrooms, bananas, and avocado to the mix). My favorite dish is a layered creation where I mix browned ground chicken or turkey with white rice that I have made using the juice from black olives instead of water and

---

[46] Balor, *Mercenary Soldier*, 84.

diced black olives. Spread out onto a baking pan, I layer sliced bell peppers, Poblano peppers, sliced bananas, avocado chunks, and altering layers of pepper jack and cheddar cheese. The meat is marinated in Bourbon peppercorn sauce and tequila lime sauce is poured over the entire dish before placing into the oven for about an hour. Served hot with a dousing of tarragon vinegar, the meal is delicious, filling, and surprisingly not fattening, but I digress…

Eating healthy is only part of the equation; you must burn off the excess fat and calories and that involves physical exercise. You will be going up against people who in turn are able to stand up against fatigue, hunger, and thirst; know how to hide and be vigilant; have mastered the art of dissembling; have learned to never fear danger; and have learned to function the same whether in day or night, mountains or desert, woodlands or jungle.[47] For now, your greatest fear is going through the day with fewer calories.

Relax; you are a long way from grabbing your AR-type rifle with the fourth-generation night vision scope and heading off to the southern border of the United States to stalk illegal aliens. That *might* come later. Presently, you need to shed some weight and beef some muscles. At least exercise will not set you back $10,000 for tactical equipment. In fact, the whole premise of this book is to get you to do extraordinary things with what is *already available to you*.

For starters, stop drinking fattening things such as regular sodas and whole milk. I lost several pounds by shifting to Coke Zero®, which, I am astonished to say, now tastes better to me than *regular* Coke®. You will further drop 15 pounds in one year simply by drinking skim milk rather than whole or 2% (the latter still bears 65% of the bad things about

---

[47] Ibid., 80.

whole milk and skim milk contains far more calcium[48]). More weight can be discharged from your bulk simply through walking. Use the stairs at work, park a bit further from the door at the store, go shopping on foot if you reside only a mile or two from the store. However you choose to do it, keep your feet *moving* through the day and the pounds will eventually come off.

Of course, before you begin *any* strenuous exercise regimen – and, eventually, you will be pumping iron, running lengthy distances, and otherwise conditioning yourself to break bones with little effort – you need to consult a physician to figure out what your particular limitations are.[49] Until you move more into aggressive training, simply use what Mother Nature has provided you with. Learn to use your *natural environment* to condition both your muscles and reflexes.

Treadmills, stair climbers, etc. not only prevent you from conditioning your *balance*, they also prevent you from coordinating your tactical mind with your environment. When you walk and run, you should be *listening* to the sounds of both your body and your location so that you can learn to dismiss the former and extract threats from the latter. This means, people, do _not_ listen to your favorite tunes on your iPod® while exercising. Why would *anyone* in his or her right mind intentionally flood their ears with noise while they are jogging alongside the road?

If you want to survive within this world of ours, you must *always* pay attention to your 360° sphere of personal awareness. What this means, is that as you drive along State Highway 33 you are constantly aware of what rests not only in

---

[48] Loren W. Christensen and Wim Demeere, *The Fighter's Body: An Owner's Manual: Your Guide to Diet, Nutrition, Exercise and Excellence in the Martial Arts* (Wethersfield, CT: Turtle Press, 2003), 115-116.

[49] Mark De Lisle, *Special Ops Fitness Training: High-Intensity Workouts of Navy SEALs, Delta Force, Marine Force Recon and Army Rangers* (Berkeley: Ulysses Press, 2008), 18-19.

front and behind you, but to the sides as well. That deer you hit last year should not have come within 100 meters of your vehicle before you notice its presence. All of a sudden plowing into a 200-pound buck at 80 m.p.h. is *not* going to keep you safe in this world. Now back to exercising...

Your entire body-mind "soul" must work *together* and therefore you cannot segregate physical exercise from work or learning from all other activities. At home, when you need to go upstairs, *sprint* up the steps (being extra cautious if you still have carpet on the steps). A trick that I learned from Sara, rest her precious soul, was to exercise while doing mediocre chores around the home. Listen, we all have to do boring things around the house every day, such as vacuuming the floor, raking the leaves, doing the dishes, or scrubbing the bathtub. We can build muscles while doing these omnipresent tasks. Practice stretching whenever you rake the leaves or sweep the floor. Do the "wax on, wax off Grasshopper" routine from *The Karate Kid* whenever you scrub the floor or the bottom of your moldy bathtub. *Always plan physical conditioning whenever you have to do physical activities!*

The entire principle of cross training is such that all of your muscles are interconnected and, should you ever have an arm or leg within a cast, for example, the strengthening of your uninjured appendage will benefit the disabled limb. Therefore, whenever you do your walking, take advantage of the asymmetrical environment of hills, curves, bumps, and other obstacles to fortify your sense of balance. When you run, alternate your rhythm by adding short bursts of *speed* in with your jogs. Learn to *sprint* even after you have run for several miles. Try never to permit repetition to become habit unless you are, say, conditioning your quick-draw instinctive shooting techniques by developing muscle memory.

Improvisational exercises can do wonders as well. While you are awaiting an email or telephone call, use the armrests of your office chair to lift your body upwards several times, building your arm muscles in the process. When near a doorway, use the aperture for isometric exercise. *Any* use of a stationary object to press against utilizes your own body weight to great advantage.

The use of small, ten-pound dumbbells will strengthen your arms immeasurably, even if you only do a few reps per day while watching television (*always* the news, or historical documentaries on war, international affairs, and military tactics!). Hold a weight in each arm as if you were carrying your rifle. This will condition you to bear your firearm for extended periods without fatigue.

Swimming remains the *single greatest exercise* of which anyone can partake. In Hawaii during my more youthful Navy days, I struggled to run a mile per day. After six months of scuba diving, I was able to dash off ten miles per day and sprint the final 300 yards along the pier faster than I had ever been able to run previously. If you are fortunate to live near the water – a lake, a river, or the ocean – *take advantage* of the situation. If you own a pool or even have access to one at a school or fitness club, then *spend more time swimming* than within any other physical activity.

These represent the most *miniscule* of suggestions, as this book was never meant to provide an all-inclusive training doctrine. Plenty of valid options in this regard already exist. It remains *your fundamental responsibility* to discover how to turn yourself, not as much into Rambo, but less as Gomer Pyle. That said, you will never go far into life if you insist upon waiting for *others* to indoctrinate you. An individual can be pointed into the correct direction, sure, but he or she must take the necessary steps to reach whatever destination he or she desires. Otherwise, a boot in the buttocks simply becomes a kick in the ass and *that* rarely does the woefully recalcitrant any good.

The next chapter will require you to be in your best condition – both mentally *and* physically. Because of this, *you* must accept – as always – the responsibility for initiative. Sadly, our society has grown accustomed to *others* making decisions for us, but it was not government, nor faith, nor education that convinced our earliest ancestors to depart Equatorial East Africa. It was good, old-fashioned *curiosity* fueled by a grand helping of basic need.

### Concepts to Remember:

- Success comes only from effort.
- *Everyone* needs improvement.
- People bore better conditioning and endurance when fitness technology did not exit.
- Lack of discipline remains the greatest obstacle towards good health.
- As with combating terrorism itself, exercise requires a lifestyle commitment.
- Exercise should not be scheduled; it should be *subliminal*.
- A healthy diet need not be painful or distasteful.
- Why are you *not* exercising while you read these words?

# 5. MARTIAL ARTS & SCIENCE

Primal warfare represents a field where people just love to go at each other, one-on-one with their bare hands. Therefore, you will ultimately have to learn to defend yourself with little more than what God has already provided you. Selecting a suitable hand-to-hand training program is a little dicey to say the least. Personally, I have qualms over practicing for something that I would rather dispense with a .45 ACP round. Then there are the many martial arts techniques that bear more resemblance to fencing than actual kill-before-you-are-killed physical combat. You will need to select a program that stresses self-discipline, preparation for physical contact and engagement, speed and coordination of mind and body, and tactics.[50]

What you do need to develop is the ability to launch into attack from *any set position* and respond to *any* threat. Frankly, you cannot do that if you waste precious moments going into a series of preconfigured stances. You will be dead long before you even think of announcing, "On guard!" Your need to develop a strong martial arts capability is to kill or subdue an enemy should the need ever arise, *not* to score points from a cynical judge or an appreciative audience. Therefore, you need to become *digital* in your actions. On, off. Kill and destroy or pack the kids off to school. *Nothing* in-between. You are either the calm, pleasant family man or you are the most lethal mother on the planet, depending upon what situation that you find yourself within at any given

---

[50] Balor, *Mercenary Soldier*, 89-93.

moment in time.

The main thing to remember when choosing a martial arts school or instructor is to stay away from the "sports" programs. I say this because of two fundamental facts: one, a black belt only guarantees that your pants will not fall down; and two, I know of instances where female martial arts "experts" were brutally raped and their male counterparts savagely killed by *untrained* losers. You need to develop the most lethal hand-to-hand combat system that you can learn within the shortest time available. Nothing less than the most destructive weapon should ever be contained within your personal arsenal – and that includes knowledge of unarmed combat. Add to this the unnerving thought that if you *wait* until defense is required; your life may have already been effectively extinguished.

Imagine, for a moment, if you were to round a corner within a crowded shopping mall and found yourself confronted with a terrorist about to detonate a bomb. Are you comfortable enough with your chosen discipline to neutralize the bomber before he or she has had time to detonate the explosives? Or would you waste precious seconds going into some pre-packaged motion instilled within your psyche through months, if not years, of hierarchal training? If you cannot take down an assailant, however armed or sized, with one quick strike then your karate preference is a waste. Period.

Before moving onto the next chapter, I would like to discuss a few "programs" worthy of study, both personally and through appropriate, professional training. The first involves Ninjutsu – the ancient art of the Ninja and perhaps the best martial arts system for the warrior operating within the bush.[51] Diverting a bit, perhaps, from the *mechanics* involved in neutralizing an enemy, this system teaches the ability to

---

[51] James W. England, *Long-Range Patrol Operations: Reconnaissance, Combat, and Special Operations* (Boulder: Paladin Press, 1987), 255.

remain concealed and stealthy in your movements. Who needs rhino-powerful strikes when you can sneak up on your enemy, slit their throat, and haul ass away before their heart attempts another beat? Ninja – the ancient trade practiced by those who were boiled alive in hot oil if they were caught, *not* the modernistic interpretation practiced by trendy Hollywood actors and their aquatic characters – represents more of a *way of life* than nearly every other martial arts package. You would do well to study its foundations.

The next "program" of note represents the modern emergence of Mixed Martial Arts (MMA) an exploding phenomenon around the planet. Mixed martial arts, perhaps rightfully so, embodies "the most complex form of combat known to man" involving "many disciplines, including boxing, wrestling, muay thai, judo, and Brazilian Jiu Jitsu."[52] MMA is certainly not a style discovered through a few weekend lessons or gazing upon a few matches on television, but integrated into your lifelong – repeat, _lifelong_ – commitment to defeating terrorists.

The ingenuity of the style, however, remains the beauty of employing maneuvers to counter any threat's actions. Nothing that evolved from an "original bare-knuckled, no-holds-barred, tournament" can be very bad for the objective counterterrorist.[53] As a warrior, you must employ every technique imaginable to ensure your safety and the demise of your enemy. The old Soviet KGB, for example, held few qualms about producing field manuals for their Alpha teams depicting the brutal killing of American Airborne and Special Forces soldiers.[54] While the United States practiced with paper targets and hay-filled dummies, the Soviets knew

---

[52] Martin Rooney, *Training for Warriors: The Ultimate Mixed Martial Arts Workout* (New York: Collins, 2008), 11.
[53] Ibid., 5.
[54] Paladin Press, *KGB Alpha Team Training Manual: How the Soviets Trained for Personal Combat, Assassination, and Subversion* trans. Jim Shortt (Boulder: Paladin Press, 1993), 217.

*precisely* who their enemy was. Do not *ever* let civility or, today, political correctness stand in the way of vanquishing your enemies.

The third system of merit rests with the Israeli implementation of Krav Maga.[55] Unfortunately, modern *commercialized* aspects of this "program" have largely defeated its original function. If you can practice the core philosophy – that of using *any rules and techniques to survive* – then Krav Maga suits well into your overall martial package. Let attorneys and diplomats challenge rules in court; *you* need to live…by *any means necessary.*

If you are going to survive within this rapidly threatening world of ours, especially one where you are going to confront people quite willing to exchange his or her life for yours, then you are definitely going to have to develop your psychic sensitivity.[56] You may not be aware of it, but you bear the ability to detect a threat from the mere glance of a person's eyes, gauge an individual's heartbeat through your own hearing, and even decipher a person's health through the color of their skin.[57] Where you may find these capabilities "miraculous" rests because ten thousand years of civilization have distanced our minds from the ravages of the Serengeti. In other words, you would probably forget how to breathe, too, if some machine provided that service for you.

We in the modern world have simply lost our natural ways and you are going to have to find some method of getting them back. Chances are you are totally lost even within your local environment. You move through a sea of people, vehicles, thoughts, responsibilities, and aspirations and I bet that you cannot separate even one of them long enough to employ all five of your senses let alone hope to

---

[55] Garret Machine, *Israeli Security Warrior Training* (Boulder: Paladin Press, 2011), 35-36.
[56] England, *Long-Range Patrol*, 255.

nurture a "sixth".

In the bush, not being able to corral your senses is tantamount to a death sentence and death is what this book is all for delaying. At least until you are a ripe old cuss begging for the trumpets of Saint Peter. Away from the trappings of modern conveniences, which are nothing more than *distractions*, your natural senses will soon notice things that you never realized that you could detect before. You will begin to notice that cigarette smoke remains detectable from up to a quarter of a mile away if you are a non-smoker.[58] You will also be able to detect food, cooking fires, even "bathroom" provisions from several hundred meters away.[59] If you do not us toiletries – *why* would you wear cologne or perfume in the bush? – you would be able to detect aftershave, soaps, and over such "luxuries" from considerable distances.[60] Now here rests the real kicker; *you* would not notice these things without having spent a considerable amount of time within, say, the jungle, but someone who had *already* developed these senses could employ them within *your* natural environment.

That is correct; you are walking down the street through some Third World cesspool and a potential assailant can smell you, Joe Modern Westerner, coming from a mile away. You do not even have to be in Benghazi to be targeted;[61] half of the people who prey on people in crowded shopping malls stalk their victims employing these same abilities. They gauge you by your own mannerisms, predictabilities, and absentmindedness. My mother once had her purse lifted from a shopping cart as a grandchild briefly distracted her. What

---

[57] R.J. Godlewski, "Human Intelligence: Perceiving an Enemy's Thoughts," *American Intelligence Journal* 27 no. 1 ((2009): 29-37.
[58] England, *Long-Range Patrol*, 255.
[59] Ibid.
[60] Ibid.
[61] In the 2008 version of this book, I used Benghazi as a random location. Last month, on September 11, 2012, our ambassador and three other Americans were killed within that city by organized terrorists. Today, in 2014 with the release of the Third Edition, the culprits still have not been apprehended. Threats do not change.

took the thief mere seconds to achieve, cost my mother three weeks' aggravation in closing credit cards, stopping checks, etc.

You may not ever find the need to take down an armed assailant – I would not rule it out, but the odds may be in your favor – but you can certainly bet that you need to become more concealed within your environment. Therefore, while you are building your macho image through MMA, study the abilities and history of the ancient Ninja groups along with the original psychology of Krav Maga and apply them to your personal needs.

Learn to employ your hands, not as appendages or even as weapons, but as sensors as well. Use them to *see* through touch alone. Use your ears to guide you around the commonplace so that you will be able to fall back upon them if your eyes are injured or incapacitated. I was about sixteen the last time that my own eyes were 20/20 unaided, so when I finally realized that my vision was less than perfect – something hard to understand when you have not anything with which to compare your abilities – I waited until I entered the Navy before I received eyeglasses.

The world of difference was so immediately spectacular, that I protected these eyeglasses as if they were the finest china. I simply never wore them while aboard my first ship, preferring to go through eight, ten, even *forty-eight* hour shifts with limited vision rather than risk wrecking my precious eyeglasses for all-important "liberty time". This was not an easy task to accomplish, especially when you had to stand electrical switchboard watches within a 140° F. engine room and pay close attention to hundreds of gauges and dials with the closest being some several feet away (computer-control did not exist then).

When my eyes began to go bad, my hearing naturally had to pick up the slack and before long I began to *hear* the distinct tone made by the whining steam generators. After roaring at several thousand revolutions day in and day out, I could detect even the *slightest* change in speed that announced the pending loss of a generator. The change in pitch was so unmistakable, that I learned to judge my actions more by my ears than the millions of dollars of instrumentation that the U.S. Navy deemed necessary.

Later, about the time that I had reached my third warship, my insistence upon protecting my precious eyeglasses dissipated with maturity. Sweat could be wiped off, dirt could be scrubbed away, and scratches, well, nobody had yet invented a practical way of keeping scratches off lenses when working aboard a WWII-surplus vessel. Therefore, I had begun to wear my glasses just as everyone else did. However, my *ears* remained in perfect – and tuned – working condition.

When we began to lose a generator aboard my new ship, I was able to inform the machinist mates *long* before their own instruments finally informed them of the changes. I had heard the generators whine down, the unmistakable change in pitch of a turbine that was slowing. Sure enough, the generator eventually tripped offline and the machinists, who were responsible for the mechanical elements, were sent scurrying about to secure them before major damage occurred while a "mere" electrician smiled with that trademark "I *told* you guys so!" smirk of his.

To develop this same trait within yourself, I suggest spending some time going around your home blindfolded. Just sit quietly on the sofa with your eyelids closed if you are still not convinced. Before you realize it, your very own ears will begin to detect sounds and noises (there is a *difference* between the two!) that you never thought possible to hear. *That* capability may save your life someday more than punching through bricks or boards. More importantly, however, such traits prove invaluable within that other, less utilized tool of countering terrorism: Mantracking.

Tactical trackers require physical fitness, visual acuity,

astounding depth perception, strong peripheral vision, and a great deal of patience.[62] The attributes that we have just discussed – learning to "see" with our ears and judging others' intentions with our combined senses – remain instrumental in tracking threats through jungles, cities, or cyberspace. Certainly, these characteristics of honesty, perseverance, inquisitiveness, acute sensory skills, initiative, tenacity, fieldcraft, and an appreciation of the "big picture" remain required skills within combat tracking.[63] Armchair counterterrorists need not apply.

**Concepts to Remember:**
- Hand-to-hand combat remains a last resort.
- Your five senses represent your best weapon.
- Sports programs lack the ability to safeguard your life.
- Practice to kill; prepare to defend; prefer to escape.
- A combination of mixed martial arts, Ninjutsu, and Krav Maga represents your best unarmed combat preparation strategy.
- Spend a portion of your day "blind" to your surroundings.
- Spend a portion of your week isolated from your "natural" environment.
- There are *no* rules when it comes to personal survival.
- Fight your current battle as if it were your last.

[62] David Scott-Donelan, *Tactical Tracking Operations: The Essential Guide for Military and Police Trackers* (Boulder: Paladin Press, 1998), 13-18.
[63] John D. Hurth, *Combat Tracking Guide* (Mechanicsburg, PA: Stackpole Books, 2012), 3.

## 6. *COMPREHEND* THY ENEMY

Before we delve into the sinister world of terrorists and transnational criminals, we need to pause for a moment and reflect upon *who* you are as an individual. Are you reading this book simply because you desire to act macho and fantasize about traveling the world and killing terrorists? Or are you simply preparing yourself for a chance encounter with someone who might irreparably alter your life forever? If you represent the first motive, then please set this book down and find one more conducive to your barbarism. It has *never* been my intention to teach you to kill or maim. That kind of individual represents precisely *whom* we are trying to defeat. If you are honest with yourself and approach the second motive, then you *still* have to address your fundamental *humanity*. For this, we need to step further back and see how far each one of us blurs the distinction.

Consider the following scenario very carefully:

Two brutal-looking thugs are in the process of raping your wife or your young, pre-teenage daughter and you have a choice between a cell phone with which to call 911 or a .12 gauge Remington shotgun. Which do *you* choose? Tough decision, right?

I am willing to bet that the vast majority of you out there – including your more liberal-minded types – would make straightaway for the shotgun even though far more people know how to operate the cell phone. This leads directly to another question: *what* to do with the gun once it is within your hands? I will hazard a guess and say that roughly 90% of the population will only *threaten* to shoot or otherwise command the individuals to cease and desist. The remaining 10% would probably shoot the rapists anywhere from the chest on upwards.

Myself? I would take out their kneecaps. This little gruesome action would serve two distinct functions. First, it would keep them alive just long enough to think. Second, it would give them something about which to think. Of course, my brief reflection upon the darker side of human nature was not meant to send the squeamish hauling off to the nearest trash receptacle to vomit. My intent here itself served two purposes. First, it provided you an honest perspective of my natural, *gut reaction*. This is important; all humans grow aggressive during moments of extreme prejudice, as politicians are wont to say. Secondly, and more importantly, I presented a strong case for educating yourself on *what* to do, *when* to do it, and what to *do it with* for whatever situation you may find yourself confronted. In other words, *learning* – that despicable word that most of us leave behind in high school or college and university classrooms.

My scenario thus serves another profound purpose; the "choice" inherent within the above scenario represents strictly a *classroom*-type problem. In reality, *no one* should even consider the cell phone for it would do very little to *prevent* the rape from actually taking place. Your actions must be instantaneous; your thoughts spontaneous. Both the shotgun and the cell phone simply represent *tools*, but only one would work well within that terrible situation.

So *where*, precisely, would you find the shotgun, you ask? Well, if the studious could imagine the .12 gauge shotgun shrunk down to a .45 caliber pistol and the preparatory would place it within a belt or shoulder holster, then the entire scenario *could* work out to satisfaction for the consciously trained. This takes foresight, yes, but also requires one to learn. For instance, how did you determine that a .45 round would be more practical than, say, a 9mm? What type of ammunition did you have loaded into your pistol in the first place? How much *realistic* practice and training did you place into using said firearm?

Next, you had to have considered *where* you would have placed your shots to ensure that the rapists were taken down without harming the victim or innocent bystanders. Far more importantly, *what* should you be doing *now* once you had saved your wife or daughter (hint: the police are initially going to characterize *you* as the immediate threat)? And you thought that adults had very little to learn about life.

The truth is, sadly, *everything* that you have probably learned since birth ill-prepares you for your new battle against terrorists and other hardened criminals. This is not to say that you have wasted your life – indeed, many things that you have already learned or experienced provide you with a distinct advantage over others – just that your mental and emotional disposition remain tainted by Western culture. It just represents the way that we are – for now.

Our brains must be *rewired* to accept conditions that remain quite unnatural and detrimental to our survival. Thoughts such as "give your money to the thieves; your life is far more important than mere material possessions" cloud our judgment due to their convincing rationale. Yet, human evolution matured away from the plains of Equatorial Africa where "giving away" things required for survival meant certain extinction. Back then, our ancestors fought back lest they starve and today our subconscious mind struggles to teach us these lessons from, perhaps, millions of years of trial and error.

At their most primal level, threats are perceived to be just that – *threats* – and we are thus forced with only the four possible options of which we have already spoken. Those that fight or flee remain around for another day whereas those who bear a definite need readily vanquish those that submit or stand transfixed in posture mode. Eventually, those that continuously flee come upon a situation where flight is blocked and those that fight may come across a more formidable adversary. It remains understood, therefore, that the *survivors* of the bunch are those who *continually evolve as fighters*.

*Time for your personal rediscovery…*

Music, I hear, represents the universal language. Whether this statement remains valid or not, I just know that it still represents many *dialects*. For example, by temperament, I am a 1960s/1970s rock and roller. There is just *something* about the raw power of the J. Geils Band that propels me towards new heights of creativity, for instance. Yet, as I wrote the original version of these words, I was surrounded by the mystical sound of the Benedictine Monks of Santo Domingo De Silos' Gregorian chant. I found their ageless "medieval plainsong" soothing and beneficial in my own art of the written word.

What this says about me, of course, is that I am neither rigid nor predictable within my mannerisms. In other words, I am very much a complicated individual who cannot be defined through stereotypes. I find this to be quite apropos – being a proponent of combating terrorism requires one to be simultaneously compassionate and lethal. The sheepdog that can thump his hind leg against the floor when being scratched behind the ear, but still sink his fangs into a much larger foe should the need arise.

You cannot be a simpleton to wage war effectively. Neither can you afford to remain predictable or live according to established patterns. This remains the fundamental reason why classroom learning leaves much to be desired. I personally know of honors students who fail miserably within the real world environment. Why did they do so well in school and yet collapse miserably outside the classroom environment? Because their minds were conditioned along the rote-learning methods of academia and therefore had their thought processes hardwired into understanding the expectations and formulas of classroom predictability.[64] I know of *few* if any academic institutions that really, *truly* change their methods of instruction from one semester to another.

You, on the other hand, cannot take such things for granted. September 11, 2001 happened because we could not imagine airliners flying into crowded office buildings. Yet, when a B-25 bomber had inadvertently crashed into the Empire State Building back on July 28, 1945, more people should have considered 'what if?" Still, we sat and watched dumbfounded when a bunch of young Arab men perpetrated the most heinous crime imaginable. We have not changed much in the interim, either.

The difficulties in changing patterns abruptly remain because we notice such changes instantaneously – our subconscious learning process at work. It is the same whenever we move into a new home or perhaps just visit a friend or relative. Those strange, quirky sounds at night that keep your mind attempting to understand that that is "foreign" to your experiences. Within your own humble abode, you are constantly acknowledging the furnace, the water heater, the wind, settling, or a host of other normal occurrences that experience has long since translated as insignificant. You do not notice these things because they have already been filed away as *unimportant* before your conscious mind even has the time to investigate them.

Much the same rests with your learning processes – you do not learn anything new *unless* your daily routine is

---

[64] Robert D. Steele, *Human Intelligence: All Humans, All Minds, All the Time* (Carlisle, PA: Strategic Studies Institute, 2010), 12.

abruptly inconvenienced. That is, you do not learn unless you are forced to discover the "new". Simply sitting around a classroom table playing paper football with your friend while the professor's back turns away is not gaining credible knowledge of *anything*. In the *outside* world with the situation involving a corporate environment, you would never really know if your lackadaisical efforts to remain amused were not being recorded by your company's hidden security cameras. Best remain focused from the moment that you first open your eyes in the morning.

Since your primary objective remains to survive an encounter with terrorists, you need to structure your knowledge acquisition within a more profitable manner that forces you to *learn* rather than forever being *educated*.

Let us begin with the simple task of taking notes – a usual method of recording information whether within a training environment or the activities of your daily professional life. Chances are that you write down notes in the same manner as you read – here in America, that means writing from left to right and from top on down. Unfortunately, because of the nature of the human mind, you will subconsciously determine that the *first* things that your eyes come across represent the most important. Suppose, however, that *something* noted towards the bottom right of your page contained valuable information that would ultimately save your life?

In order to force your mind to consider *all* information regardless of how large your piece of paper is, begin taking notes through inconsistent methods of writing. Write both diagonally and vertically. Use different sizes of script and colors of pens. Forego colloquial English in favor of shorthand scribbling – decipherable symbols that you have invented for just such a purpose. Arrange your notes within a haphazard manner all around the page. What this does, is force your mind to concentrate on *every* note written down, as you are required to *stop, look, and pay attention* to what does not appear "natural" to your lifelong process of reading. You retain the pertinent information because you have not ruled it out as "unimportant" before you actually realize what it represents.

Now that you have managed to shake yourself free of conventional learning processes – and truly *knowing* how to learn – you can proceed applying that ability towards your counterterrorism role. You must begin to *understand* the threat aligned against us and formulate an educational plan that will provide you with distinct advantage over them.

Your enemies, of course, represent terrorists, but can you adequately *define* terrorism? Many an academic and political soul have fought over what truly constitutes terrorism and terrorists for years, but for the purposes of this book, we shall agree with the following definition:

> "I believe that a consensus can be found that would categorize terrorists as private or state-sponsored groups operating largely outside the control of the national military whose fundamental goal is to intimidate people and their governments into recognizing the group's ideologies and/or religious beliefs through the coordinated use of indiscriminate murder, torture, and the destruction of private and public properties, especially that which will achieve a great deal of attention by local and international media organizations. Therefore, this is how I generally define terrorists and anybody who aids them in any manner whatsoever is a terrorist supporter."[65]

We can further refine our terrorist enemies by revealing them to represent Islamist jihadists or narco-traffickers, but we must always be extremely cautious that parties allied with their

---

[65] R.J. Godlewski, *Integrated Technical Warfare: An Organizational Guide to Creating a Corporate Counterterrorism Force* (Houghton Lake, MI: Road Sailor Books, 2006), 91-92.

hatred of us do not buck the trend as it were.[66] We simply do not know from whence a threat to our existence may come and therefore we must always understand that terrorism remains a tool, and *not* specifically a defined group of individuals. This requires examining terrorist models from the historical context.

### The Socialist/Anarchist Model

For convenience, two similar models have been combined. Their commonality in the form of "anti-democratic" purpose leads to their indistinguishable classification on our part as well as their equally common historical lineage. That is, both socialists and anarchists desire to dismantle the status quo in an effort to change the *existing political system* of their target body. Of the two, only the socialists generally care enough to anticipate an alternative to the current condition of their host nation. Still, they are not beyond using the services of anarchists to quicken such a change much as Adolf Hitler did during the 1930s. The 21$^{st}$ century version of this could quite possibly represent the various "Occupy" movements that began cluttering Wall Street for perceived economic injustices. *Who* exactly swells within the phantasmal cloud of popularity may not always represent the purported cause itself.

Anarchists, for their part, are more liable to orchestrate their trade via "Propaganda by Deed"; that is, by exercising the "Philosophy of the Bomb".[67] They simply want to destroy cultures by disrupting peace and security. The detonation of a bomb represents the ultimate ambush; it catches people completely off guard, generates terror at the speed of the expanding gases, and increases the "emotional distance" between the perpetrator and the innocent civilians they often

---

[66] Ibid., *xiv*.
[67] Walter Laqueur, *The Age of Terrorism* (Boston: Little, Brown, and Company, 1987), 48-51.

kill.[68]

Bombs can be made so simple that a "child" could use them or they can represent super-sophisticated devices such as the Lake Tahoe Casino bomb that contained over 1,000 pounds of high explosives, 34 switches, alternative detonators, and *could not be defused.*[69] Either way, the possibilities for expanding mayhem are infinite – merely matching the sophistication of the device with the training of the individual. For their role, socialists are usually more concerned about such issues as class struggle and worker's rights.[70] Their heyday appears to have been the late 1800s and early 1900s before legitimate unionism became a standard, if somewhat archaic, fixture in the global economy. Groups such as the Molly Maguires and the Western Union of Mineworkers freely practiced "working-class terrorism" to further their aims.[71]

The rise of free trade, right-to-work capitalism, and more disciplined unions have largely capped the extreme violence of one hundred years ago though, as in many aspects of modern life, these problems merely migrated towards the developing southern hemisphere.

### The Argentine Model

What began with Fidel Castro and Ernesto "Che" Guevara in Cuba found itself transplanted in Argentina during the latter 1960s. Whereas the originators of this escalation could rightly lay claim to a "Cuban Model", I have chosen to include Argentina for the precise period between 1969 and 1979 remained unlike any other period in global history, save for perhaps the gangsterism widespread throughout Chicago

---

[68] Grossman, *Defeating the Enemy's Will*, 167-169.
[69] U.S. Government, *Federal Bomb Intelligence: U.S. Government Guide to Terrorist Explosives* (Boulder: Paladin Press, 1991), 73-74.
[70] Laqueur, *Age of Terrorism*, 52-53.
[71] Ibid., 15.

and the American Midwest during the 1920s.[72]

For a country that once quipped "more people were hurt at a Mexican wedding than in an Argentine coup d'état", the 1970s ushered in a cruel reality that the people were figuratively not in Kansas anymore.[73] The nation had dealt with both Perons, which exhibited leftist *and* rightist extremes, and a sizeable portion of their population felt that Argentineans represented the old guard for the Old World; yet what eventually happened to their country shattered these misconceptions.[74]

What *did* happen and what makes the Argentine Model so singularly represented here is that terrorism took to their country from *both sides*; from the agitators and the reactionaries. The leftist guerrillas sought to overthrow the establishment and the establishment worked aggressively to 'disappear' anyone and everyone who threatened security. Soon, the Spanish word *desaparecido* simply became a more "tasteful euphemism" for having had died under the auspices of the brutal government.[75]

Thus, when people simply "disappear" instead of die, it remains difficult to get a handle on the true level of terrorism that existed during this period within that nation, but the implications speak loudly nevertheless. The overreaction towards the locals by the security forces ensured that the people delighted in the fact that many police officers and military personnel were themselves routinely assassinated.

Soon, the frenzy included journalists, priests, teachers, and nearly everyone else in otherwise prudent public life. For all their brutality, for the untold thousands of dead, for the existence of secret prisons run by both the military and police

---

[72] Robert Cox, "Total Terrorism: Argentina, 1969 to 1979" in *Terrorism, Legitimacy, and Power: The Consequences of Political Violence* ed. Martha Crenshaw (Middletown, CT: Wesleyan University Press, 1983), 124-142.
[73] Ibid., 129.
[74] Ibid.
[75] Ibid., 128.

alike, there "was virtually no left-wing terrorist activity within Argentina" by 1980-1981.[76] Society had finally begun to tame the security forces, for the Argentines had fully believed that they were "the heirs to Western, Christian civilization" and had a most difficult time believing that their own security forces had become "more barbaric than the terrorists."[77]

What the Argentines had learned the hard way was the instrument most useful in dealing with fanatical elements; a lesson plan which society had been dealing with for ages.

### The Haqqani/al-Qaeda Model

By anyone's definition, this section could be adequately termed "The Islamist Model" and whether Shia or Sunni in origin, the implications remain the same. However, the distinction of the Jalaluddin Haqqani Network bears scrutiny, for this remains the network that fostered Osama Bin Laden's al-Qaeda and fuels jihadist activities far beyond its Afghan base of operations. Emerging from an Afghan and Pakistani insurgency group during the 1970s, the Haqqani Network (HQN) shaped al-Qaeda's trajectory throughout the region.[78]

Jalaluddin, during the Soviet invasion of Afghanistan, captured Khost and remained instrumental in piecing together "a diverse constituency of groups" between Afghanistan and Pakistan.[79] Later, during the 1980s, "Jalaluddin quickly rose to be one of the [Pakistani Intelligence Agency's] most favored field commanders."[80] More recently, the HQN serves as the Taliban's "force multiplier" strengthening the Islamist group's campaigns throughout the region.[81]

---

[76] Ibid., 131.
[77] Ibid., 129.
[78] Don Rassler and Vahid Brown, *The Haqqani Nexus and the Evolution of al-Qa'ida* (West Point, NY: Harmony Program, Combating Terrorism Center, U.S. Military Academy, July 14, 2011), 1.
[79] Ibid., 9-10.
[80] Ibid., 13.
[81] Ibid.

The connection between Haqqani, Bin Laden, the Taliban, Afghanistan, Pakistan, and Sudan underscores the fundamental support that HQN has provided al-Qaeda and, in fact, the Bin Laden group owes its very existence to Jalaluddin.[82] Nevertheless, al-Qaeda bears some unique differences that warrant discussion, despite the underlying support (and guidance) of HQN. Think of al-Qaeda – and its various post-9/11 emulators – as mere proxies of Jalaluddin and HQN.

Al-Qaeda's master plan represents a three-pronged attack against the West. These three phases of their "guerrilla war" are as follows:[83]

Phase One: Attrition. During this phase, the jihadists plan to 'hit and run' against their targets, allowing spectacular strikes in order to gain attention from the media and generate an increase in recruiting efforts. Examples include 9/11, which drove a rift between the U.S. and Saudi Arabia, the attack upon the U.S.S. Cole and, undoubtedly, the recent attacks in Benghazi on September 11, 2012;

Phase Two: Relative Strategic Balance. During this phase, the jihadists seek an equilibrium that will permit them to set up base camps, hospitals, Shari'a courts, broadcasting stations, etc. within newly conquered, or in their terms, "liberated", locations. This possibly represents what has transpired throughout the Middle East/Northern Africa (MENA) following the so-called Arab Spring uprisings;

Phase Three: Military Decision. During this phase, the jihadists announce their 'arrival' within smaller cities and

---

[82] Ibid., 30.
[83] Norman Cigar, trans. *Al-Qa'ida's Doctrine for Insurgency: 'Abd Al-'Aziz Al-Muqrin's A Practical Course for Guerrilla War* (Washington: Potomac Books, 2009), 92-102.

the countryside where they will shift their base camps and receive support from the broader Islamic community. Specifically, the jihadists plan to "intimidate" their enemies by stressing the inevitability of their surrender, during which *Shari'a* courts will be established to try (read that, *convict*) everyone who had rebelled against Islam.

Without a doubt, the Islamist game plan can be witnessed throughout the world today, as they secretly move into virgin territory, force the indigenous agencies to "overreact", thereby applying the "victimization" card all the while waiting for an opportunity to emerge victorious and convict those who tried to stop them. A sizeable portion of this effort, it would appear, utilizes the concept of *al-Taqiyya*, or deceit in order to blend in or deflect charges of subversion and hostility.

### The Religious Model

Local populations swelled with those suffering disorientating and rapid change. Citizens felt that their rights had been eroded and that justice was not on their side, so they became frustrated with what they perceived to be authoritarian regimes that did not preserve local traditions based exclusively upon God's Law as outlined within bona fide religious texts. The Middle East today? No, German-speaking Europe during the 16th century.[84]

Religion today has become a blasé subject for some and an outright taboo for others. It comes therefore, as no surprise that most are fully disconnected with the intimate role that religion plays within global civilization. We have come to accept that "freedom of religion" means, specifically, that we

---

[84] Ralph Peters, "Rebels and Religion: How Fighters become Fanatics" *Armed Forces Journal* (January, 2007), 29.

are free *not* to have to deal with the subject rather than the more traditional interpretation that we are allowed to either choose our religious beliefs or choose not to accept any religious beliefs. This fine line between choosing *not* to practice religion and empowering us to *deny* religious expression completely (which rests as something of a religion in its own right) remains a significant flaw within modern society.

With 92% of the world's population believing in theism and 84% subscribing to some form of institutionalized belief, it remains decidedly difficult to understand how some people can still conduct their lives without acknowledging that the rest of the planet remains overwhelmingly spiritual in nature.[85] This has grave consequences in regards to the study of terrorism and its current practitioners.

Faith today, especially within the Christian West, leaves much desired. Our ancestors *lived* for the afterlife; today we tend to fabricate terrestrial religiosities.[86] Formal religion has become a *mere part* of our lives, along with football, tractor pulls, dance music, and shuffling the kids off to grandma and grandpa so that we can enjoy a break from parental responsibilities. Religion used to *be everyone's life* – in Europe and elsewhere – but we contemporaries tend to mock those who exhibit even some of these traditional values.

Religion – of whatever flavor – enables the *true* believer to undertake the most extraordinary tasks. It represents what makes a mortal man, such as the aforementioned Simeon Stylites, live upon a stone pillar for most of his life and it is what makes impressionable teenagers strap on a bomb vest and detonate it within a crowd of wedding guests. It also defines the raw hatred of a Klan member and the selfless love

---

[85] According to www.adherents.com, roughly one-half of the 16% "non-religious" people still believe within a divinity. The rest comprise atheists, agnostics, and others.
[86] Kreeft, *Everything you ever wanted to know*, 193

of a soldier who throws his body upon a live grenade. 'It' is *all* about faith and how that individual person *perceives* his or her particular faith.

Religion is not simply about *believing in God*. Tens of millions of Americans alone "believe in God", but the relationship usually ends as soon as the statement leaves his or her lips. For example, there are probably some 80 million "Roman Catholics" within the United States today, but few, if any, strongly subscribe to Vatican doctrine. As soon as you hear, for instance, a politician spout affiliation with the Church *and* acceptance of the "right" for an individual to choose an abortion, then you have a gross misrepresentation of faith from that individual. The Church requires that the "*disciple of Christ must not only keep the faith and live it, but also profess it, confidently bear witness to it, and spread it: 'All however must be prepared to confess Christ before men and to follow him along the way of the Cross, amidst the persecutions which the Church never lacks.'*"[87] This includes politicians who are required to use their profession to spread the Gospel to all men.

Nevertheless, in truth, "it often remains the *minority* which remains faithful to a particular ideology or religion."[88] This thesis illustrates in two ways. One, the vast majority of Catholics within the United States who support, say, abortion, gay marriages, married priests, etc. are in error of the Church's 2000+ years of established doctrine. On the other hand, the "silent majority" of the Muslim world knows "very little about the teachings in the Quran and sunnah that give Muslims the right to use terrorist activity as a war method against the enemies of Islam."[89] There is little confusion, therefore, that the vast majority of Muslims act much as do the

---

[87] *Catechism*, #1816.
[88] Godlewski, "Latte Intelligence", 77.
[89] Mark A. Gabriel, *Journey into the Mind of an Islamic Terrorist: Why they hate us and how we can change their minds* (Lake Mary, FL: FrontLine, 2006), 183

vast majority of Roman Catholics; both remain secularists at heart and understand very little about their faith's official doctrine.

Where problems occur, rests with the vast gap between the beliefs of devout Catholics and devout Islamists. No self-respecting Catholic (or even Protestant) would endorse indiscriminate violence as a means of entering Heaven. In fact, the earliest Christians willingly went to the lions or suffered burning alive as garden torches rather than offer harm towards another living soul. If we are, therefore, incapable of understanding a religion that has been part of our civilization for two thousand years, how much *more* incapable are we of understanding religions that are newer (or, at a minimum, newer to our nations)?

Religious terrorism represents far more than just Muslim extremists. For example, "historians report that there is a tradition of violence among the Sikhs."[90] The Thugs subscribed to a devotion to the goddess Kali.[91] Rarity does not preclude the potential and even mainstream religions, such as Hinduism, Buddhism, as well as Christianity bear the potential for misuse by individuals or cults. Today, faiths of which we may not even consider as "religious" in nature, such as environmentalism, progressivism, etc. fuel hatred and destruction amongst some adherents. The qualifier remains whether or not the devotee believes in his or her cause as *greater* than legitimate public law instituted by a free and unhampered electorate.

### The Narco Model

In fullest disclosure, this represents less of a model

---

[90] Laqueur, *Age of Terrorism,* 233.
[91] Ibid., 13-14.

than as an entire way of life. Narcotics "cartels"[92] employ terrorism as simply a tool, one of many they employ against those who seek to stop them as well as against competition. Nevertheless, no single group of individuals bears more violence upon innocent souls than the narco-cartels populating Latin American and elsewhere. For our purposes, we need to address several key factors. First, the most notorious narco-paramilitary group remains *Los Zetas*; an infamously deadly group founded by 31 deserters from Mexico's Airborne Special Forces Groups and originally aligned with the Gulf Cartel.[93] According to the U.S., *Los Zetas* represents the most violent, sophisticated, and threatening private army in Mexico.[94]

Already, such cartels – and the armies they employ – have warned U.S. agencies that the groups' snipers will target any off-duty (or sans uniform on-duty, apparently) law enforcement officers who attempt to thwart the drug trade, *even if those officers are in, say, Arizona*.[95] Besides the obvious, any narco-induced collapse of the Mexican economy threatens to turn the border region into a form of "Waziristan, U.S.A." as millions of potential immigrants flee northward to avoid the turmoil.[96]

To understand their influence, one must know the *architecture* of narcotics trafficking groups, organizations that parallel Islamic jihadists in evolution. DTOs exist within a series of loosely interconnected social networks involving both

---

[92] Some researchers suggest that the term 'cartel' represents a regrettable misappropriation of verbiage, "sacrificing conceptual and empirical clarity for stylistic convention". See Kenney, "The Architecture of Drug Trafficking", 233. Nevertheless, this book continues to employ the term for convenience, as most readers assume the definition to represent a coordinated criminal group seeking to profit from broad narcotics production and distribution.

[93] Hal Brands, *Mexico's Narco-Insurgency and U.S. Counterdrug Policy* (Carlisle, PA: Strategic Studies Institute, May 2009), 8.

[94] Ibid.

[95] Mark Spicer, "Mexican Drug Cartels: The Growing Threat of the Sniper Attack", *Journal of Counterterrorism & Homeland Security International* 16, no. 4 (2011): 50.

[96] Kan, *"Narco-Refugees"*, 25-29.

'wheel' and 'daisy chain' structures.[97] They cultivate *métis* – an ancient Greek term that describes the broad application of skills and experiences that professionals employ to adapt to a constantly changing human and natural world.[98] Métis is often the result of brainstorming or sensemaking sessions wherein various participants within the smuggling operation gather to (largely) informally discuss what had worked within the past or not.[99] This information exchange permits the DTOs to engage within competitive adaptation that serves as a force-multiplier against counternarcotics groups and competitors.[100] It will not be long before the Islamic model merges with the Narco version to create a single social network of transnational criminality.

### The Lone Wolf Model

Some individuals just want to kill and/or maim as many of us as they can for an infinite number of perceived grievances. On May 18, 1927 Andrew P. Kehoe loaded his truck with dynamite and rusty machinery parts and drove to a Bath, Michigan school on the outskirts of Lansing and killed 38 children and 6 adults, including having had bludgeoned his wife back at their ranch.[101] His grievance? He was upset at the taxes levied upon him in order to pay for the tiny hamlet's new school.[102] It *still* ranks as the worst school massacre in U.S. history. Theodore "Unabomber" Kaczynski and Eric Rudolph of the Olympic Park bombing in 1996 both held anti-institutional grievances and evaded arrest for years while they

---

[97] Michael Kenney, *From Pablo to Osama: Trafficking and Terrorist Networks, Government Bureaucracies, and Competitive Adaptation* (University Park, PA: The Pennsylvania State University Press, 2007), 30-32.
[98] Ibid., 53.
[99] Ibid. 60.
[100] Ibid., 104-108.
[101] http://freepages.history.rootsweb.ancestry.com/~bauerle/disaster.htm. Accessed October, 2012.
[102] Ibid.

plied their murderous trade.

Making matters worse, lone wolf terrorists such as the "workplace violence" shooter down at Fort Hood, Texas, Nidal Hasan, may or may not be acting alone. Even the 1995 Oklahoma City bombing undertaken by Timothy McVeigh and Terry Nichols bears credulous influence from World Trade Center (WTC) 1993 terrorist Ramzi Yousef.[103] That Nichols and Yousef ended up in Cebu City, Philippines during the same time and the OKC bomb design proved remarkably similar to the original WTC bomb remains far more than interesting coincidence.[104] Remember, in nature, even lone wolves often emerge from packs.

### The Tempered Glass "Model"

One cannot assume that terrorists will continue to meet definitive expectations, as the trend already proves apparitional. Narcotics groups evolved by necessity away from hierarchal bureaucracies into diverse social gatherings where individuals and independent businesses shield the industry from direct attack by governments and post-Bin Laden al-Qaeda certainly followed this track. In this regard, perhaps, a singular "model" exists that must be considered by individuals analyzing terrorism.

When a plane of tempered glass shatters, the product disintegrates into a multitude of harmless beads that scattered into every conceivable direction. Where blocked by barriers, these pellets congregate into clumps of material, otherwise they continue until momentum ceases and they come to a stop as individual beads. What had been conveniently contained within a neatly designed and dimensional pane of glass now occupies an indeterminable field where, depending

---

[103] Peter Lance, *1000 Years for Revenge: International Terrorism and the FBI: The Untold Story* (New York: ReganBooks, 2003), 308-318.
[104] Ibid.

upon specific location, "clean up" remains imperfect at best.

This "tempered glass" scenario represents the present status of al-Qaeda and drug trafficking organizations following the death of Pablo Escobar and the dismantling of his subsequent Cali competitor. The taking down of the notorious drug kingpin in 1993 and the post-9/11 attacks against al-Qaeda both forced remnants of each specific organization to behave in the manner of glass beads scattering upon an uneven surface. Some members have regrouped into recognizable clumps whereas some individuals regained footing as independent – and far more dangerous, perhaps – entities. Both cases require attention from *anyone* comprehending combating terrorism.

### Concepts to Remember:

- Terrorism represents a tool, although some criminal groups remain defined as "terrorists" by their indiscriminate use of such a tool.
- Terrorism models can *aid* in categorization, but such classifications remain more for convenience than value.
- Terrorists – as *criminal* groups – focus more upon terroristic methods rather than ideological barriers. That is, terrorists will join forces with *whoever* can assure their objectives rather than avoid associations that violate that group's core values.
- Religious, political, and social preferences do *not* dismiss the presence of terrorist groups, who can arise from any religious or political persuasion.

# 7. COMPREHENDING THYSELF

Never had I become such a controversial figure than when I had begun to preach the need for individual involvement within the fight against terrorism. My steadfast opposition towards *all forms* of abortion seems to have generated little concern. My pro-American stance has created few enemies amongst my foreign readers. My overtly religious writings had caught very little attention, even from those who dismiss God. Even my openly Roman Catholic evangelization simply amuses my Protestant and Muslim friends.

However, as soon as I announced that fighting the war against terrorism remains *everyone's business*, I quickly became something of a renegade within society. *Why?* Undoubtedly, because whenever you mention combating terrorism, one of only three thoughts immediately comes to the mind of most individuals:

1. Combating terrorism remains the sole domain of Hollywood action flicks detailing the infamous (or fantastical) exploits of Navy SEALs, Delta Force, or some sinister CIA-based group;

2. Combating terrorism remains a police function to be handled *solely* by certified peace officers, federal agents, or teams of international diplomats;

3. Terrorism is merely a minor disturbance that does not deserve the attention that it receives.

R.J. GODLEWSKI

It is, and *always* has been (since at least ~1981), my personal belief that *everyone* must be involved within our national security, regardless of our profession or training. This is not an easy subject to consider, but just as the world's Muslims could not believe that nineteen Arab men could "fool the CIA" in order to pull off the September 11, 2001 attacks, we cannot do the opposite and rely *exclusively* upon our government or our military to protect us.[105] As ex-CIA operative, Robert Baer, wrote: "And what had saved the city I was living in? Not the CIA. Not the FBI. Not the air force or navy or marines or army. But the raw courage and determination of a fistful of average Americans."[106] The passengers of United Airlines Flight 93, in my estimation, represent the truest embodiment of independent counterterrorism for they alone saved the nation's capital.

Ignorance of events, whether from Arabs or Americans, is most definitely *not* a good thing. Why, therefore, are we predisposed to being "shocked" when horrible things happen? Why are we, as a nation, so *incapable* of protecting ourselves without relying upon our taxpayer-financed services? Because the fear of aggression has become our "mother's milk".[107] We simply are not reared to become *warriors* anymore. That we might actually be *bred* to fight is never considered amongst even our "danger loving society."[108] We remain so appalled at our fellow man's desire to terminate us that most of our species would willingly go to our deaths rather than raise a single hand in defense of our own lives. Do not believe me? Remember, what is the *first thing* that a police officer or public official will tell you to do during a robbery or burglary? "Give them what they ask for. Your life is worth more than mere material possessions." Ever notice the news lately? Have you

---

[105] Gerges, *Journey of the Jihadist*, 183.
[106] Robert Baer, *See No Evil: The True Story of a Ground Soldier in the CIA's War on Terrorism* (New York: Three Rivers Press, 2002), 268.
[107] Balor, *Mercenary Solider*, 102.

ever considered what would have happened if *all* aircraft passengers on 9/11 had fought back?

There remain many instances – again, just pay attention to the news – where some spunky gas station attendant or retailer thwarted a robbery, even against armed assailants, by fighting back. These do not represent isolated incidents, either. The main reason that the police tell you to give up is that they do not want to be sued by saying that, in many cases, merely giving up your prized possessions will *not* save your life. People rob you because they *believe* that they can get away with it. Just notice the drop in crime for communities with concealed-carry permits. If you are afraid to die, then chances are so is the thug trying to rob you blind.

On September 11, 2001, Osama Bin Laden and his al-Qaeda organization did not believe for a moment that the United States would respond in the way that it did.[109] We did respond, however. Only 75% of the planes diverted to strike us on that infamous day succeeded in reaching their target; the fourth plane's passengers *fought back* Everyone aboard United Flight 93 knew they were going to die, but they chose to fight back in order to save their fellow citizens from a fate far worse than death. *Of what great debt do we now owe them?*

By not taking a stand – a realistic and actionable one, that is – against terrorism you have become your own worst enemy, which is why I have chosen to write a complete chapter on knowing *yourself*. It is when we, the common folk of this planet, determine that our lives are only worth as much as whatever someone *else* decides that it is worth do we allow ourselves to become truly worthless. Part of the reason is that we fear placing this fragile life on the line. The rest of it is undoubtedly because we are afraid of placing our *rights* on the

[108] Grossman, "Defeating the Enemy's Will", 151-153.
[109] Gerges, *Journey of the Jihadist*, 202-211.

line. I, for one, have chosen to end this interminable dance with fate. *My* life is worth defending and worth defending, possibly, to the death. What say you?

## Know Thy Territory

To know simply *who* is trying to kill you is definitely not enough. You must fully understand the geography of terrorism as well; and this, friend, means pretty much the entire planet. Chances are, however, that you get lost on your way to the local supermarket. Fortunately, unlike the terrorists themselves, knowing the planet, the nations that surround it, and the overall texture of the humanity that contaminates its surface, is a straightforward process. I say this because physical and political structures do not evolve nearly as fast as the human minds that conceive of them.

You therefore possess more time in which to analyze Geospatial Intelligence – the combination of using computer software and analytical methods with terrestrial or geographic datasets – but, at this stage, you need not be so advanced in your counterterrorism activities or your preparation for survival.

What you need to do, for the moment, remains to concentrate on nations and their subcultures. You need to understand things such as national leadership, ethnic groups, local religions, key industries, principal alliances, etc. The following comes from the U.S. Army's *Guerrilla Warfare and Special Forces Operations FM 31-21* field manual (9/1961). Using core data retrieved from the CIA's World *Factbook*, you can adapt these data recommendations pursuant to your files on each nation or region depending upon how diverse your target group remains:

## *General Area Study*

### General

*1. Political*

- Government, international political orientation, and degree of popular support;
- Attitudes of identifiable segments of the population toward the United States, its allies and the enemy;
- National historical background;
- Foreign dependence and/or alliances;
- National capitol and significant political, military and economic concentrations.

*2. Geographic Positions*

- Areas and dimensions;
- Latitude and climate;
- Generalized physiographic;
- Generalized land utilization;
- Strategic location:
  - *Neighboring countries and borders;
  - *Natural defenses including frontiers;
  - *Points of entry and strategic routes;

*3. Population*

- Total and density;
- Breakdown into significant ethnic and religious groups;
- Division between urban, rural, and/or nomadic groups:
  - *Large cities and population centers;
  - *Rural settlement patterns;
  - *Areas and movement patters of nomads.

*4. National Economy*

- Technological standards;
- Natural resources and degree of self-sufficiency;
- Financial structure and dependence upon foreign aid;
- Agriculture and domestic food supply;

- Industry and level of production;
- Manufacture and demand for consumer goods;
- Foreign and domestic trade and facilities;
- Fuels and power;
- Telecommunications and radio systems;
- Transportation – U.S. standards and adequacy:
  *Railroads;
  *Highways;
  *Waterways;
  Commercial air installations.

*5. National Security*

- Center of political power and the organization for national defense;
- Military forces (Air, Navy, Air Force); summary of order of battle;
- Internal security forces – summary of organization and strength;
- Paramilitary forces: summary of organization and strength.

**Geography**

- Climate. General classification of country as a whole with normal temperatures, rainfall, etc., and average seasonal variations;
- Terrain. General classification of the country noting outstanding features, i.e., coasts, plains, deserts, mountains, hills and plateaus, rivers, lakes, etc.
- Major Geographic Subdivisions. Divide the country into its various definable subdivisions each with generally predominant topographical characteristics, i.e., coastal plains mountainous plateau, rolling, heavily forested hills, etc. For each subdivision use the following outline in a more specific analysis of the basic geography:
1. Temperature. Variations from normal and, noting the months in which they may occur, any extremes that would affect operations;
2. Rainfall and snow. Same as above;
3. Wind and Visibility. Same as above;
4. Relief:
   *General direction of mountain  ranges or

ridge lines   and whether hills and ridges are dissected;

    *General degree of slope;

    *Characteristics of valleys and plains;

    *Natural routes for and natural obstacles to cross-country movement;

5.    Land utilization. Not any peculiarities, especially the following:

    *Former heavily forested areas subjected to widespread cutting or dissected by paths and roads; also, the reverse, i.e., pasture or waste land which has been reforested;

    *Former waste or pasture land that has been resettled and cultivated – now being farmed or the reverse (former rural countryside that has been depopulated and allowed to return to waste land);

    *Former swamp or marsh land that has been drained; former desert or waste land now irrigated and cultivated; and lakes created by dams;

6.    Drainage. General pattern:

    * Main rivers, direction of flow;

    *Characteristics of rivers and streams such as current, banks, depths, type of bottom and obstacles, etc.

    *Seasonal variation, such as dry beds and flash floods;

    Large lakes or areas of many ponds and/or swamps.

7.    Coast. Examine primarily for infiltration, exfiltration, and resupply points:

    *Tides and waves; winds and current;

    *Beach footing and covered exit routes;

    *quite coves and shallow inlets or estuaries;

8.    Geological basics. Type of soil and rock formations (include areas for potential landing zones for small aircraft).

9.    Forests and Other Vegetation. Natural or cultivated.

    *Type, characteristics and significant variations from the norm and at the different elevations;

    *Cover or concealment-density, seasonal variation;

10.           Water. Ground, surface, seasonal and potable;

11.           Subsistence. Noting whether seasonal or year-round:

           *Cultivated – vegetables, grains, fruits, nuts, etc.

           *Natural – berries, fruits, nuts, herbs, etc.
           *Wildlife – animals, fish, and fowl.

## People

The following sub-outline should be used for an analysis of the population in any given region or country or as the basis for an examination of the people within a subdivision as suggested above. In all events particular attention should be given to those areas within a country where the local inhabitants have peculiarities and are at considerable variance in one or more ways from the normal, national way of life.

- Basic Racial Stock and Physical Characteristics. (1) Types, features, dress, and habits. (2) Significant variations from the norm;

- Standard of Living and Cultural (Education) Levels. (1) Primarily note the extremes away from average. (2) Class structure (Degree of established social stratification and percentage of population in each class);

- Health and Medical Standards. (1) Common Diseases. (2) Standards of Public Health. (3) Medical Facilities and Personnel. (4) Potable water supply. (5) Sufficiency of medical supplies and equipment;

- Ethnic Components. This should be analyzed only if of sufficient size, strength and established bonds to constitute a dissident minority of some consequence. (1) Location or concentration. (2) Basis for discontent and motivation for change. (3) Opposition to majority and/or to the political regime. (4) Any external or foreign ties of significance;

- Religion. (1) Note wherein the national religion definitely shapes the actions and attitudes of the individual. (2) Religious divisions. Major and minor religious groups of consequence;

- Traditions and customs (Particularly taboos.) Note wherever they are sufficiently strong and established that they may influence an individual's actions or attitude even during a war situation;

- Rural countryside. (1) Peculiar or different customs, dress and habits. (2) Village and farm buildings – construction materials;

- Political Parties or Factions. (1) If formed around individual leaders or based on established organizations. (2) If a single dominant party exists, is it nationalistic in origin or does it have foreign ties? (3) Major legal parties with their policies and goals. (4) Illegal or underground parties and their motivation. (5) Violent opposition factions within major political organizations;

- Dissidence. General active or passive potential, noting if dissidence is localized or related to external movements;

- Resistance (Identified movements). Areas and nature of activities, strength, motivation, leadership, reliability, possible contacts and external direction or support;

- Guerrilla groups. Areas and nature of operations, strength, equipment, leaders reliability, contacts and external direction or support.


### Enemy

- Political. (1) Outside power (Number and status of non-national personnel, their influence, organization and mechanism of control). (2) Dominant National Party. Dependence upon and ties with an outside power; strength, organization, and apparatus; evidences of dissension at any level in the party; and the location of those areas within the country that are under and especially strong or weak non-national control;

- Conventional Military Forces (Army, Navy, Air Force).
    (1) Non-national or occupying forces in the

country:

(a) Morale, discipline, and political reliability;

(b) Personnel strength;

(c) Organization and basic development;

(d) Uniforms and unit designations;

(e) Ordinary and special insignia;

(f) Leadership (officer corps);

(g) Training and doctrine;

(h) Equipment and facilities;

(i) Logistics;

(j) Effectiveness (any unusual capabilities or weaknesses).

(2) National (indigenous) forces (Army, Navy, Air Force) and repeat (a) through (j) above;

- Internal Security Forces (including border guards).

(1) Strength and general organization, distinguishing between non-national and national elements:

(a) Overall control mechanism;

(b) Special units and distinguishing insignia;

(c) Morale, discipline and relative loyalty of native personnel to the occupying or national regime;

(d) Non-national surveillance and control over indigenous security forces;

(e) Vulnerabilities in the internal security system;

(2) Deployment and disposition of security elements:

(a) Exact location down to the smallest unit or post;

(b) Chain of command and communication;

(c) Equipment, transportation and degree of mobility;

(d) Tactics (seasonal and terrain variations);

(e) Methods of patrol, supply and reinforcements;

(3) The location of all known guard posts or expected wartime security coverage for all types of installations, particularly along main LOCs (railroads, highways, and

telecommunications lines) and POL lines;

(4) Exact location and description of the physical arrangement and particularly of the security arrangements of all forced labor or concentration camps and any potential POW enclosures;

(5) All possible details, preferably by localities, of the types and effectiveness of internal security controls, including checkpoints, identification cards, passports and travel permits.

### Targets

The objective in target selection is to inflict maximum damage on the enemy with minimum expenditure of men and material. Initially, the operational capabilities of a guerrilla force [AUTHOR'S NOTE: Translate into counterterrorism force] may be limited in the interdiction or destruction of enemy targets. The target area and the specific points of attack must be studied, carefully planned and priorities established. In general, targets are listed in order of    priority:

- Railroads. (1) Considerations in the selection of a particular line – (a) importance, both locally and generally; (b) bypass possibilities; (c) number of tracks and electrification. (2) Location of maintenance crews, reserve repair facilities and equipment. (3) Type of signal and switch equipment. (4) Vulnerable points – (a) unguarded small bridges or culverts; (b) cuts, fills, overhanging cliffs or undercutting streams; (c) key junctions or switching points; (d) tunnels. (5) Security systems.
- Telecommunications.
- POL.
- Electric Power.
- Military Storage and Supply.
- Military Headquarters and Installations.
- Radar and Electronic Devices.
- Highways.
- Inland Waterways/Canals.

- Seaports.
- Natural and synthetic gas lines.
- Industrial plants.

At this point, you are probably overwhelmed over the amount of information that the foregoing *General Area Study* requires. Not to worry, the vast majority of it will not apply to you. However, I have included it for several reasons, all of which I consider extremely important to your role as *active* counterterrorist. First, this remains a *lifelong* pursuit that you are undertaking and as the world and your adversaries evolve, you are going to have to develop your own intelligence database of existing and potential threats to your nation and, most especially, to our way of life (particularly if you do a great deal of overseas travel).

Secondly, the advent of the Internet and high-speed data communications provide you with the *opportunity* to establish a rudimentary intelligence *network* that represents a fundamental need in tracking and eliminating terrorist threats. What was once required of a complete battalion to undertake can now be achieved by small groups or individuals who consciously set aside the time and initiative to track down some of this information. Finally, just because *you* have not determined a need for collecting this information regarding, say, Iran, Pakistan, or Somalia, do *not* believe for a moment that your terrorist enemies are not collecting such information about you or your own nation and its allies.

In fact, knowing *what* enemies might be seeking about your own nation falls under the discipline of *counterintelligence* and your efforts may be most helpful to your federal and military forces – which represents why *you* are getting involved within counterterrorism activities in the first place. Therefore, for those of you who do a great deal of travel abroad, start educating yourself regarding the places that you tour and for those of you eternally planted within your own country, start seeking out those who wish to harm you there.

There is one subject more important than perhaps just knowing about the world's people and nations, however. The knowledge remains interconnected, but the effort is no less demanding or important. You have to understand the *languages* of this vast world of ours.

## Talk the Talk

Unless you can communicate in a language other than your own, you remain at a distinct disadvantage when it comes to protecting your family and friends – not to mention your country and global security. Nationalistic appeal aside, there rests no legitimate reason to be singularly linguistic in today's day and age of globalization.

Whether the Polish I learned as a kid owing to my own heritage; the French that I studied rather poorly while in high school; the Japanese that I absorbed while deployed to Japan for three months; the Tagalog that assured some semblance of survival while visiting Subic Bay; the brief Korean picked up while stopping at Pusan; the Brazilian Portuguese studied for my trip into the Amazon; the Spanish required for jobs where I was the *only* one who spoke English; the Russian that I picked up at Michigan State; the Ukrainian of my good friend; or the Arabic that I have studied both academically and professionally; I have myself learned how quickly one can not only be required to deviate from their native tongue, but how easy it can be to learn enough of another language to survive. And I did not even bring up Farsi, Hebrew, or Amharic.

With the availability of technology today, anyone can begin to practice a new language of his or her choosing. You have, for instance, Rosetta Stone® software, videos appearing on YouTube, and even Defense Language Institute programs available for purchase via eBay. The conscientious citizen will be able to learn to read, write, and speak a new language with unheard of rapidity.

For combating terrorism, you need to become familiar with at least one of the following languages – Arabic, Farsi, Spanish or Russian, depending upon your location. With the way the world is going, I would also recommend the dialects surrounding Afghanistan and Pakistan, perhaps Central and Northern Africa as well. *Any* knowledge will further your cause to delve into tracking the beasts and keeping yourself alive during the process. Remember, however, that 99% of what you will undoubtedly be doing remains within your own backyard.

This is, after all, not an all-inclusive manual; it represents a guidebook to steer you into the right direction. A book designed to work with the free *Independent Counterterrorist* training modules that can be updated and tailored as needed towards rising threats. Your fundamental desire upon completing this book remains the ability to formulate something of warrior intent within your personality. It represents 'Boot Camp' of a sort and much training and personal conditioning lies ahead. Again, you *do not want* your adversaries understanding what you know. هل تفهمت آلان؟

## Walk the Walk

When handsome "youthful and ruddy" David pledged to fight 6'6" Goliath of Gath for King Saul, the king thought that the kid was absolutely nuts: "*You cannot go up against this Philistine and fight with him, for you are only a youth, while he has been a warrior from his youth.*"[110] Undeterred with this bit of generational prejudice, David simply replied, "*Your servant used to tend his father's sheep, and whenever a lion or bear*

---

[110] 1 Samuel 17:33, *NAB*

*came to carry off a sheep from the flock, I would go after it and attack it and rescue the prey from its mouth. If it attacked me, I would seize it by the jaw, strike it, and kill it.*"[111] So much for the timid little shepherd boy...

We *all* know how the story ended. David used his trusty sling to embed a stone into his opponent's forehead rendering the much larger individual dead – at least as dead as one could ascertain without a modern medical examiner present – and then finished his adversary off with a beheading from Goliath's own sword (which effectively eliminated the need for any modern medical examiner). David went on to become king, chose whatever wife he wanted (even if she was already married at the time), and fathered a son whose eventual wealth, judgment and prosperity would make *any* parent damn proud of him.

There are several morals in this tale that apply directly to you. First, you do not need the best technology available in the world to defeat your enemy. You just need the most effective technology *available to you*. Secondly, you do not have to be as large or as well trained as either your enemy or the forces too inept to fight them on their own accord. You just need proficiency in whatever technology *you* use. Finally, and this is by far the most important lesson, David knew how to ensure that his enemy was dead by decapitating the giant. We do not need to become *that* barbaric, but we must become that *thorough*. Just as with David, when we fight our enemies, we must ensure that they remain *incapable of attacking us* without the need for a licensed medical examiner to determine their status.

Far too often within our society, we try to *civilize* our response to threats and the only thing that we manage to do is to ensure that our enemies live to fight again on another day. Consider former President Jimmy Carter who had reduced

---

[111] Ibid., 34-35.

U.S. covert operations capabilities by 40% from 1977 to 1979 to avoid having the CIA conduct "dirty work."[112] Islamic "students" stormed our embassy in Tehran (as well as the one in Pakistan) in 1979. Perfect timing. Carter's own national security advisor noted concerns over "the astonishing lack of information" following the Shah's collapse and the subsequent seizure of our sovereign territory.[113] The Islamic Republic of Iran and its tyrannical mullahs have been a thorn in our side ever since and the current liberal administration in Washington appears content to repeat these same errors. Makes you wonder just how differently things would have been today if we had just gone ahead and bombed the Ayatollah back into the Stone Age, right?

Instead, we evolved into a nation where the U.S. Army spent $100 *Billion* developing its new Future Combat Systems (FCS) program, but showcased the technology within a lame, politically-correct video where one child was saved from a virus and five "clownish terrorists" were apprehended by we 'good guys'.[114] Nobody bothers to tell our government and our citizenry "war means fighting and fighting means killing."[115] Our nation might be obsessed with "kindness" but if you use it as a platform on which to protect your family, you will end up on the losing end. Period.

In this regard, we can remember the words written by the Prussian general Carl von Clausewitz"

> "Kind-hearted people might of course think there was some ingenious way to disarm or defeat an enemy without too much bloodshed, and might imagine this is the true goal of the art of war.

---

[112] Stephen F. Knott, *Secret and Sanctioned: Covert Operations and the American Presidency* (New York: Oxford University Press, 1996), 174.
[113] Ibid., 175.
[114] Ralph Peters, "Killing with Kindness: Political Correctness Infiltrates the Army" *Armed Forces Journal* (December 2006), 28.
[115] Ibid., 30.

> Pleasant as it sounds, it is a fallacy that must be exposed: war is such a dangerous business that *the mistakes which come from kindness are the very worst* [emphasis added].[116]

You will *die* as a counterterrorist operative if you engage within kindness to the exclusion of your martial capabilities. The U.S., as but one example of misguided "kindness", often kills a great many innocent people within its wars because of sloppy intelligence and targeting.[117] It remains perfectly okay to be considered a brutal savage as long as *your* efforts do not produce collateral damage.[118] The United States can no longer accomplish this – if it ever could.

Think of it what you may, but our national defense remains predicated upon transitory politics. What one administration may enforce today, another may deny tomorrow and vice versa. This means that the safety of your loved ones boils down to what is currently rising within the polls – unless *you* alone act. You must, I cannot state often enough, dedicate the *entirety of your life* to combating terrorism even if shared with your other responsibilities. Inasmuch as one cannot expect to breathe *only* 85% of the time, one cannot contribute only one or two days per week or "only" ten or twenty years to survival. It must represent an "all or nothing" proposition and you must continuously train as such.

To formulate some strategic thinking within your day, I suggest patterning your life after the color code system developed by retired Colonel Jeff Cooper of the U.S. Marines:[119]

---

[116] Carl von Clausewitz, *On War* eds. and trans. Michael Howard and Peter Paret (Princeton, NJ: Princeton University Press, 1976), 75.
[117] Balor, *Mercenary*, 230.
[118] Ibid.
[119] Erik Lawrence, *Tactical Pistol Shooting: Your Guide to Tactics That Work* (Iola, WI: Gun Digest Books, 2005), 14-16.

## Color Code for Personal Awareness

White. This represents the state of being "Fat, Dumb, and Happy". You are very relaxed; completely unprepared for anything. You may be in this condition within your own home particularly if you own security systems, guard dogs, and even weapons. Attacked while in "white mode" and you probably will not survive one minute.

Yellow. Here you are relaxed, but with a non-specific alert. No immediate threat exists, but you remain alert eying all possibilities. No one can approach you without your being aware of him or her. You are not anticipating any trouble, mind you, but are prepared for it. You are within this condition, say, whenever you drive your vehicle, checking your mirrors frequently looking for obstacles even though they may not be there and wearing your seatbelt even though you do not anticipate any collisions.

Orange. This represents a *specific* alert status. *Something* – a person, a vehicle, a situation – grabbed your attention. There might be a very simple and innocent reason for your heightened concerns, such as a stranger approaching you to inquire of the time, but you just want to be on your guard before you shift back down into Condition Yellow.

Red. This represents the "fight is on!" mode that you dread experiencing, but spent your entire life preparing for, the situation where your mental "go" button is pressed. Someone might be approaching you with a gun, a raised baseball bat, or wielding a knife. This is where your "kill or be killed" posture comes into play even if it might not be ultimately exercised. A simple "If you do 'X' then I will do 'Y' algorithm. You are not 100% positive as to what your adversary will do, but you sure as hell know what *you* will do when the situation escalates.

It remains understood that you should never allow yourself to be caught "pants down" in Condition White. Even while sleeping, your conditioned, subconscious mind still functions; just make certain it understands what is "home" and what is "strange". Remember, "A simple plan, well-rehearsed and violently executed, offers the best chance for success."[120] I just love the *violently executed* phrase. It goes neatly with what Napoleon once spoke of regarding the concept of speed: *"I may lose a battle, but I will never lose a minute."*

Thus far, within this book, we have discussed the imperative to fight, the power of faith in combat and survival, the need for conditioning yourself both mentally and physically – even to the point of developing something of the "ancient ninja" within your life. We examined your learning habits and how to improve them, as well as a bit about your various terrorist enemies and their supporters. We discussed delving into knowing as much about the physical and social world around us and presented a case for learning a few of the languages of this world. Most importantly, we just finished discussing the need to "walk the walk" instead of merely stating that we wish to do something about protecting our loved ones and ourselves.

Ultimately, there may come a point within your life when all of the preventative measures in the world fail and you find yourself confronted with the proverbial "do or die" situation. Herein, you will discover once and for all whether you possess what it takes to literally take another's life (or at least gravely wound them). I will not make any pretense about it; it remains a thought that scares even the most hardened of souls. *You* can only determine what happens when that situation arises. Armies have "fought" for centuries trying to figure out ways in which to make their soldiers fight for real, but the truth remains that only a very small handful of individuals actually see combat. It is not very different today than it was during the American Civil War when 27,574 muskets were recovered

---

[120] Ibid., 17.

from the Gettysburg battlefield – 24,000 were loaded; 12,000 of these were loaded more than once; and 6,000 of the multiply-loaded firearms had from three to ten rounds jammed within the barrel (one weapon was even loaded 23 times without having been fired!).[121]

What this says about us is that we fear "looking weak" nearly as much as we fear fighting itself. We will load guns repeatedly without firing a single shot, but we will die at least looking as if we are truly fighting. Fortunately, technology has eliminated such redundancy, but only *you* can actually squeeze the trigger upon another human being. This is probably a question that you have asked yourself a million times in the past, especially whenever you have watched a Hollywood 'action' movie on television or in the theater.

Myself, I guess that I have never had this problem. I was about seven years old when I shot my older brother in the leg with a pellet gun. I was even younger when I drove a pencil deeply into his leg, leaving a gruesome blemish to this very day. I have said it once and I have said it a thousand times since – I have never, *ever* injured another living soul that did not *deserve* it. ☺

### Concepts to Remember:
- Combating terrorism requires a blood oath on your part.
- You require actionable intelligence within your targeting.
- *You will die* if you approach this way of life haphazardly.
- A sound mind and a sound body represent the foundation upon which you are to build your counterterrorism efforts.
- Do not fear harming individuals, but remain deathly fearful of harming *innocent* human beings.
- Do not permit *any* encounter with another individual go without challenge.
- Remember, "mistakes which come from kindness are the very worst."

---

[121] Grossman, "Defeating the Enemy's Will", 158.

# 8. WEAPONS OF THE INDEPENDENT

When avoidance and patience have failed and the need arises for personal defense, you can count on the availability of an infinite variety of weapons – both improvised and purchased – to aid in your particular situation. We shall discuss each category and implement my personal recommendations. Each one of you will have your own thoughts, your own budget to work with, and your own physical limitations. More importantly, this chapter inherently favors (and remains directed towards) American citizens who, by virtue of the U.S. Constitution, specifically the Second Amendment, possess the right to keep and bear arms. Therefore, as with *everything* about combating terrorism, you must study on your own, seek out further resources, and employ sound judgment and common sense.

My recommendations herein thus merely reflect what particular image I bear of an independent counterterrorism agent; your needs and requirements reflect upon your particular situation, motivation, desires, finances, and applicable laws. We all have our "dream list", even our "bucket list", as well as our "permissible list". As the world grows more dangerous and the rest of us slowly catch up to fact, our own laws may begin to reflect upon this fundamental need.

For example, again, at the time of this new writing, the concealed-carry map remains fluid with most states providing some form of right-to-carry. Illinois remains the sole holdout with several recent court decisions in favor of armed citizens, and a handful represent "may issue" states, meaning that they want to ensure that you meet all of their requirements before they even consider handing out your carry permit. These, too, have lost significant court battles recently. Three states, Arizona, Vermont, and Alaska, permit concealed carry *without* a permit. Most states that issue permits recognize other states' concealed carry permits, meaning that fellow residents of Michigan, say, can drive all the way to Florida armed.[122]

Now that we have whetted your appetite for what remains to come, it is to our distinct advantage to begin our discussion of weapons with the most accessible of all – those that God has given to you. There will come a time when, all the permits and rights in the world aside, you will find yourself within a critical situation where *no* weapons are available and you must defend yourself accordingly.

## Unarmed Combat

We have already discussed your martial arts training; this section leans more towards *targeting*. Even if you should, God forbid, find yourself confronted face-to-face with an armed assailant, not all is lost – you *do* have options. While your body may not be made of stone and your hands quite delicate instruments of manipulation, the same holds true for your attacker. That he or she may possess a knife, a firearm, even a broadsword does not in any way, shape, or form increase the strength of their vulnerable points.

Consider the following scenario:

> A man stops you leaving your ATM machine at midnight, leveling a 9mm automatic at your midsection with his right hand and demands the cash that you just withdrew from the machine. What do *you* do?

---

[122] The 2012 version of *Mini-Manual* dispensed with both the conceal-carry map and the list of state reciprocity laws as that information was dated from 2006. Where laws are considered, it remains best not to suggest them within print and

Most people would probably collapse to the ground, losing their money in the process. A few others might go catatonic, fumbling around hysterically for the money that they already possess within their hands. At best, *all* of the above would be hoping, subconsciously, that *someone else* would be courteous enough to place a phone call to the community's *post event* responders.[123] Remember, it is the police and the politicians who have told you to capitulate and then *wait* for the appropriate authorities to arrive. They say this because they know that when *you* need them, they are most likely serving someone *else* a great many miles away.

In fact, in a ~2008 shooting in Detroit where a little seven-year-old *handicapped* girl was shot *several* times protecting her mother, it took *three calls to 911 before the police eventually showed up!* The first call was disconnected; the second call merely led to the emergency operator telling the caller that there were no units available in the area to respond – *remember that line folks, remember it well* – and the third call, which finally got some reaction out of Detroit's finest, had to be placed by a gas station attendant himself. Besides the sheer bravery of that little girl – now *there* is someone who would make a great counterterrorist! – this story shows that help, even within a major U.S. city, is never, *ever* going to respond to your expectations.

So what *might* you do in the situation outside your ATM machine? For starters, how about:

> In a *split-second,* you strike his right wrist with your right hand pushing his arm towards your left, holding his wrist firm within your grip. Immediately, you use your left hand to bend the gun backwards – employing the pivot point of his wrist, which you are currently holding – taking it away from him or

---

recommend that the reader explore the pertinent laws of his or her state. For broader information, please visit sites such as http://www.usconcealedcarry.net.
[123] Lawrence, *Tactical*,10.

knocking it towards the ground. *Simultaneously*, you deliver a *powerful* kick to his groin disabling the attacker.[124] If he does not cease and desist after you have acquired his gun, you might consider shooting the creep between the eyes, but I do not want you to turn bloodthirsty on me. That is definitely _not_ what this book is about. However, if you are still agitated and fumbling with the gun, give him one more sound kick to the groin. That will make you feel a little better and keep him from running away.

The foregoing may not have been amongst your first thoughts, but it should have been amongst your first options. Unnecessary delay in action may result in the loss of your life. Did you, for example, actually believe that the thug would not have killed you after you would have given him your money? Times are changing; people are becoming more vicious and no decent hoodlum wants a witness around who can identify him. Will the above action work for *you*? Impossible to tell, but that is not the point. I have merely outlined a *possible response* where, perhaps, thirty seconds ago you possessed none. I have merely outlined one possible response to one possible threat scenario in order to present the case that you *do* possess options, even when confronting the worst possible situations.

More likely than not, the creep with the gun did not expect you to do anything other than what *he* wanted you to do. There is, after all, no longevity in robbing people known or expected to be armed themselves. Consider, Goliath; he did not expect tiny little David to unleash a rock upside his head. As powerful as he was; as terrible as his reputation was; as sharp as his sword was, big bad Goliath was felled by one well-placed shot from a young rock slinger – something of a forerunner to today's professional snipers, to be sure.

---

[124] Steve Crawford, *Deadly Fighting Skills of the World* (London: Brown Books, 1997), 14-15.

There remains another, perhaps less enjoyable, thought for you to consider within the foregoing ATM scenario. Your body has only a few extremely vital target spots – we will discuss wound ballistics in a bit – and even at close range, you present a very small target. Forcing the robber's gun away, even by a small degree, removes his line of firing away from your most vulnerable midsection. Even if he were to pull the trigger, the more that you can deflect his gun away from you, the *better* for your chances of survival. I, for one, would rather take a shot in the arm or leg than one into the gut.

Whatever the situation, there remains one key factor to be discussed. While the gunman may not be expecting you to fight back, *you*, on the other hand, must be prepared to do *something* to restore the situation back into your control. This means practice, training, forethought, and dedication to your life. Your rapid *actions* – not hysterical reactions – undoubtedly will catch most criminals off guard. They simply expect average citizenry to capitulate and fork over their money and possessions. This means that events will turn into your favor while your opponent goes into "*Damn, I did not expect them to do that!*" mode. Time is the most precious commodity of all, which is why, during our discussion on martial arts, I warned you to stay *away* from reliance upon "sport" techniques that merely indoctrinate you into fairness and civility.

Therefore, for example, should you ever successfully disarm a gun-carrying opponent and drop them down onto the ground, go ahead and stomp on their face a couple of times. It will teach them a lesson and you will walk away a bit calmer for the effort. Sure, the police will probably arrest you. Sure, the courts will probably try you. Sure, the bastard's own legal team will probably sue *you*. Nevertheless, were *they* around to help when needed? Probably not. Besides, ask for a trial by a jury of *your* peers. They probably hate the system as much as you do.

The reoccurring theme here is not to be brutal for its own sake. Contrary to popular opinion, I do not lead such a barbaric life myself. In all probability, I am one of the nicest individuals that you could ever meet. I am intelligent, have a very spontaneous wit (that takes quite some time getting used to! ☺), and possess a deep, rational concern for my fellow human beings. That said, I would like to provide you with two stories that bear strong parables. The first involves an episode while I was assigned to my third ship in the Navy, an Adams class destroyer. We were being repaired within the shipyard at that particular time and I, having just had the entirety of my large toenail removed (before the anesthetic took effect), was serving 'light duty' aboard the barge that substituted as our electrical shop.

Four of us were in the shop on that particular day, my first-class petty officer, my second-class petty officer, me, and a huge brute that was eventually dishonorably discharged on cocaine possession or something. Anyway, this person was about three sizes bigger than I was and decided that he wanted to thump his finger on my exposed bad toe, delivering a shock of pain whenever he flicked against the wounded appendage. At first, I did nothing because I erroneously concluded that my superiors, who were seated a very short distance away, would do something about it. By his fourth thump, I had had enough, supervisors present or not, I reached up, grabbed the jerk by the throat, and threw him backwards over his stool.

The absolute glare within my eyes must have frozen him because he did not flinch a muscle while I read him the riot act for what seemed about five minutes. After that day, my "Goliath" and all of his doper friends would not lift a finger to rile me. Lesson learned: I *will* defend myself, so even if I may appear docile, do *not* let my demeanors deceive you.

The second story involves my old dog, an Australian Cattle Dog, or Blue Heeler. He had a peculiar habit of covering his dog food dish with doilies, unwashed clothes, or anything else that he could find within reach. He even liked to bury his "business" atop a small bush or back up against a tree rather than defecate out in the open. Despite this, he had been known to drop a 2,000-pound bull that had become rather troublesome for a local rancher.

Several years ago, my dog had broken loose from the yard (he always had a bit of Houdini in him) and spent an all-nighter away from the house. His festivities ended when he was attacked by another dog and nearly died from the encounter. The veterinary assistant replied that he had undoubtedly learned his lesson and would no longer be a problem. The very next day, my dog snuck out again, probably to go after the sonofabitch (quite literally termed, I might add). I am the *same* way.

No, I do not like it whenever people glorify death and killing, but I am not afraid to defend myself either – even if, like my dog, it means finding me lying near death on some farmer's field. Should I ever be attacked I, too, will go after my adversaries for no other reason than to make them *pay* for their crimes. And I possess a *very long-term* memory. This might mean legal restitution. It might mean armed encounters on the other side of the planet should they remain a threat to innocent bystanders. This is the way that it *has* to be when dealing with terrorists and transnational criminals. We have to keep *pounding* at them until *we* are safe enough to go back to living our quaint little lives *wherever* we choose to settle down.

As I have said, the human body remains a very frail instrument and this aids us when confronting threats unarmed. There remain several vulnerable spots to target:[125]

- Trachea, neck, larynx, neck arteries, neck veins,

---

[125] Haha Lung, *Assassin! The Deadly Art of the Cult of the Assassins* (New York: Citadel Press, 1997), 107-121.

R.J. GODLEWSKI

esophagus;
- Eyes, nose, mouth, chin, ears, jawbone, skull-spine juncture;
- Base of the skull, seventh vertebra, kidneys, renal artery and vein;
- Hips, stomach, thigh, calf, shin, top of foot, all joints and articulations;
- Rectum, groin.

Some of these areas work better with knives and other weapons, but do not underestimate the power of your hand once you have conditioned it through your physical-martial program. You will possess the option of applying the kick, the punch (or strike), place pressure or attempt strangulation, pull, bite, and use leverage against the joints and articulations. The *types* of injuries that we can instill upon our foes range from several pain or trauma (broken bone, kick in the groin, etc.) to knocking them out (punch in the chin, etc.) to even death (broken neck) – all with our *bare* hands and feet.

Perhaps the easiest targets for you to seek are the groin (kicking, hitting, squeezing), the nose (fist punch, hammer blow), top of the foot (stomping), the shins (kicking), and the kidneys (karate blow, fist punch, kicking) all of which cause severe trauma within your opponent, though intense pressure on the testicles can lead to death. The two targets that can *permanently* incapacitate your attacker are the back of the neck (karate blow, hammer blow) and the clavicle hollow of neck (severe pressure, stabbing). To be effective, however, you must exercise and practice your punches, strikes, etc. to gain the strength needed for when the time should come. Fill up an old duffle bag with sand or heavy clothing; perhaps use an old chair as your punching bag. Just wrap your hands up so you do not suffer any injuries during practice and whale away on your target, concentrating on coordinated actions delivering beefy punches and kicks and not just wimpy throws of flesh.

## Weapons of Opportunity

Rarely will you find yourself in a position where there is *nothing* around that you cannot turn to your advantage. I have already mentioned how a spunky five-year-old can bring down his older brother with a pencil. Relax, he is fine. He grew up to be one of the top law enforcement officers in the country within his chosen specialty. We do not talk much today...

Anyway, the point remains – quite literally – that anything that does possess a nice, sharp point can be applied to devastating effect upon an individual. A pencil, a pen, an umbrella end, even a piece of stick can be used to pierce the human body.

What you need to do is make a *habit* of examining things around you that may come into play at any given moment. If you are attacked in a restaurant, do you throw coffee into the assailant's face and then follow up with the knife and fork to his eyes? Or do you need the knife and fork to buy time in order to reach the boiling pot of coffee?

While shopping, do you use your heavy shopping bag against his body or your purse (if you are a woman) upside his head followed by a swift kick to the groin? Outside in the parking lot, do you gouge his eyes out with your keys or do you have a sock loaded with coins that you can employ as a very *lethal* club? Perhaps you reside out West and have a big ol' buckle on your belt that you have learned to swing with all of the effort of a champion roper?

Truck drivers generally carry some form of billy to thump their tandem wheels in order to check for flat tires. Unfortunately, we were never allowed then to carry weapons and even our clubs were considered illegal if kept in the cab. However, many enterprising drivers kept short brooms in their cab that had – you guessed it – very stout handles that had a habit of loosening with ease. They simply improvised to suit their need. Myself, when I ran refrigerated trailers, I keep a long meat hook (borrowed from hauling swing beef) that I ostensibly used to pull my fifth wheel pin when dropping trailers off. In reality, it served as a weapon and with practice, I found that I could take out a hand-sized chunk of wood from trees or two-by-fours with ease. Imagine its use upon a person.

You need to venture back into traditional semantics when being unarmed meant being *limbless*. You must constantly gaze about you and see things, not as utensils or commodities, but as potential weapons of opportunity. Do *not* terrify your wife or girlfriend during dinner by salivating over the thought of bashing your neighbor's brains out with the deep-dish pizza pan. Just understand that the pizza pan is *there*, is fairly heavy, and easy to grasp (although probably *very hot*) and file that knowledge immediately away into your primed subconscious mind.

Improvised weapons – or weapons of opportunity as I like to call them – are just that; things that *might* aid in your survival situation should the need ever arise. Seek them out, but do not go overboard unless the situation warrants. Then, throw literally *everything* that you can at your target.

## Edged Weapons

Knives can represent far more than just utility devices; they can be powerful instruments of destruction. Nevertheless, for all of their practicality and convenience, I do not recommend their use beyond, perhaps, keeping your hands and weapons of opportunity from being required. Fighting with knives represents something that just cannot be learned through a few weekend sessions, as they are not "point and shoot" devices such as guns. And, God forbid, please *do not even think about throwing knives* at your enemy. If you miss –

and you probably will as moving targets are hard to hit even with firearms – then you have simply given your weapon to someone who, if he did not before, probably wants to kill you more than ever now.

For a knife to be used as a lethal instrument, the most proper technique applied is simply to thrust the blade into your opponent's most vulnerable spot as quickly and as frequently as possible. Ideally, this remains the kidneys, which, incidentally, provides a much faster method of incapacitating a person than those quirky cover-the-mouth-and-slit-the-throat moves seen in war movies. Someone with a throat gouged out can *still* make a sound, but if a relatively tiny kidney stone can drop a full-grown man, just imagine what a Ka-Bar® could do once thrust into one of his kidneys.

Forget fancy posturing moves pulled from silly movies such as *West Side Story*; once you realize that a grave threat exists, you should already be exercising that lovely tactic known affectionately as disemboweling your enemy. Knives and other edged weapons represent a last resort. A bit more practical than bare knuckles, perhaps, but not anything that should require your time and effort to the exclusion of firearms and avoidance. This said, I would offer a few pointers and leave the reader to investigate on his or her own.

When I drove within the household goods industry many years ago, I had once made a purchase of an awesome looking "survival knife" fashioned much like the one that became famous within the movie *First Blood*. Being required to move people into and out of some of America's most notorious cities, I felt decidedly more protected with its 12-inch blade hanging from my hip. Inside of the handle were matches, a fishing rig, a wire saw, and the cap itself contained a compass – important considerations to possess for all of those runs we made into Western and Northwestern states.

My knife was not cheap, but it was not handcrafted either. Not in the sense that some craftsman staked his livelihood and reputation on the quality leastways. The blade served its purpose as a deterrent well – people used to cross the street *against* traffic just to avoid walking near my truck when they saw it – and it sliced through boxes and packing tape efficiently. It was when I had to employ the knife within its "prying" mode that I realized just how cheesy the instrument truly was. The blade simply bent with the slightest ease. I suspect, now, that it would have bent even if it were lodged between a person's ribs. I do not mess with such inferior quality "experimental" blades anymore and it remains nonsense to employ them as a *deterrent*.

I demand a knife that can be used to serve a range of needs – cut vines in the  bush, skin a grizzly (and lower mammals), deflect an oncoming blade in close quarters battle should *that* need ever arise and, of course, penetrate an enemy's body easily and repeatedly. Naturally, some blades are better suited for some tasks than others are, so I am forced to admit some degree of compromise. For instance, a Fairburn knife is good for stabbing and even slashing, but as an overall tool, it leaves much desired. Therefore, choose any form of "combat knife", with or without a serrated edge, and you should do okay.[126]

Brand names are numerous and I suggest that you concentrate on offerings from Ka-Bar®, Ontario Knife Company, and Cold Steel®. This also leads to a discussion on other forms of *edged* weapons. Some, writing for readers in locations where firearms remain prohibited, suggest a range of weapons from swords, to axes, and even machetes.[127] Personally, I do not see the practicality of employing a broadsword half the length of my body, but if I were in the woods, desert, or jungle, I would certainly avail myself to some of the better quality tactical tomahawks out there. Even the

---

[126] For a large assortment of edged weapons, visit www.trueswords.com.
[127] Eugene Sockut, *Secrets of Street Survival – Israeli Style: Staying Alive in a Civilian War Zone* (Boulder: Paladin Press, 1995), 89-152.

terrorists fear being sliced and diced with a blade – a tomahawk simply places American tradition into the skull of a fanatical enemy. Finally, of course, a fine quality Katana sword scares the living crap out of *anyone* and makes for a great *de-*conversation piece in the office.

Nevertheless, unless you foresee a clear and demanding need to rip out someone's windpipe or pierce their lungs and heart repeatedly – which *all* long, thin, and sharp instruments are capable of doing – I would concentrate on the utility aspects of owning an edged weapon. Meaning, of course, that your blade will find its most effective use out where food, clothing, and shelter remain far more valuable rather than dispensing with a villain better dispatched with a heavy hitting bullet. Owning a knife or tactical tomahawk is no different than owning a firearm. It represents a *tool* and little more. In *your* hands, it might save an innocent life, but there are far better tools out there with which to practice that trade.

### *Handguns*

The handgun is, by far, the most practical weapon available for personal defense within the United States or other urbanized environments. Handguns come in a nearly infinite variety of sizes and shapes, from the small .22 caliber derringer revolvers on up to Wildey's .475 magnum auto pistol on through Smith & Wesson's behemoth .500 S&W Magnum hunting revolvers.

For convenience, I am going to make two rather straightforward assumptions at this point. First, you remain dead serious about combating terrorism and you are eventually going to let people know where you *actively* stand on the issue. Second, because of this, your personal safety may be more at risk than if you were some timid and shy pastor at a tiny community church. Therefore, I will dispense with making any recommendations or references to calibers not considered adequate "man stoppers" (my .500 S&W is not entirely for stopping grizzlies up close).

Furthermore, because this book is a *mini-manual* – meaning that it is "supposed" to be small and easily read within the shortest available time – I will equally dispense with the range of "my gun" versus "your gun" debates that necessarily arise from situations such as this. Manufacturer suggestions will be kept to the very minimum and caliber recommendations kept even narrower. There remains a wealth of knowledge available via the Internet and your local gun shop where you can – and *should* – conduct research on your own preferences.

Let us begin now with caliber selection for it represents the easiest to discuss. Even within the context of hunting, our society remains predicated upon foregoing stopping power for convenience. We just do not think "big" even when what we are aiming at may turn out *damn big*. Whatever living thing we shoot at, we must:

1.    Hit a vital spot;
2.    Hit that vital spot with a bullet that will hold together;
3.    Throw a large enough bullet at that vital spot in order to create a *reliable* wound channel through the target.[128]

Too many people, whether hunting man or beast, subscribe to less powerful weapons for fear of "getting kicked" by the recoil of the firearm, but end up sending round after round into their prey in order to subdue their target.[129] This is not restricted to hunting either. The durable .45 ACP cartridge was developed within the early years of the 20th century

---

[128] Ray Ordorica, "Use a Big Rifle" in *Gun Digest 49th Annual Edition* (Northbrook, IL: DBI Books, 1995), 195.
[129] Ibid., 197.

because its predecessor – the .38 – could not stop deranged Moro tribesmen in the Philippines who were hopped up on drugs. The smaller bullets (diameters measured in inches or millimeters) simply could not drop the attackers fast enough and many U.S. soldier or marine had emptied their six-shot revolvers into the fanatics to no avail; the .38 caliber service revolver was just too ineffective on maniacal subjects, such as the ones that you might encounter during the 21st century.

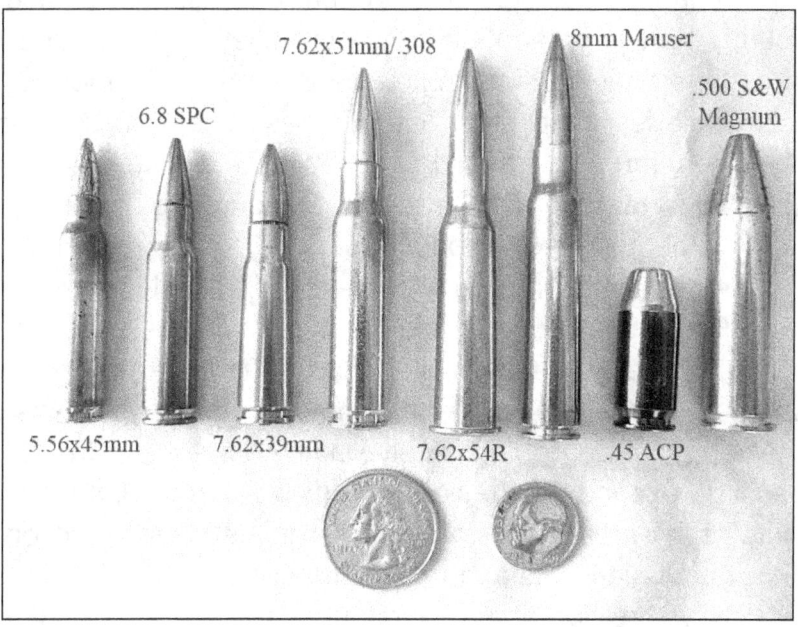

**Figure 1. Comparison of firearms cartridges.** © R.J. Godlewski.

Consider the above photograph regarding a few of the author's chosen calibers. Even a casual glance will inform you that "bigger is better" when it comes to throwing bullet weight down range at your intended target. Added to this, is the cartridge length that runs the gamut depending upon the manufacturer's specifications. For example, the 7.62mm Kalashnikov (AK-47/AKM) assault rifle round is 39mm in length, whereas the 7.62mm NATO round has a length of 51mm, and the 7.62mm rimmed (R) round used in Russian long rifles possesses a length of 54mm.

Two bullets of the same caliber may provide exceedingly different trajectories and performance, depending upon whether the cartridge is a "long gun" round used for rifle shooting at distance or an "intermediate round" employed within assault rifles used primarily for close quarter combat. Next, we have to consider bullet *weight*, measured in grains, such as my .308 Winchester bullets of 168gr or my .45 ACP pistol rounds in 230gr. If this does not sound confusing enough, there represents a range of bullet *types* running the gamut from hollow-points that expand upon hitting their target to incendiaries that burst into flames when striking solid objects on through frangible rounds that disintegrate when hitting hard targets. The reader is encouraged to read and research the numerous capabilities.[130]

At the risk of inviting argument, I will simply recommend .45 ACP for male shooters and 9mm for smaller shooters such as women. Yes, the U.S. military has shifted over to exclusive use of the 9mm, but I prefer to employ a round with a history of taking down large, aggressive attackers even if the bullet does not expand as designed (which is how 9mm hollow points have entered the fray of preferences). A malfunctioning .45 makes a bigger hole than a malfunctioning 9mm.

Now, as for actual handguns. Here, too, remains a range of choices with the best, perhaps, resting with Smith & Wesson, Beretta, Glock, Taurus, Sig, FN Herstal, Heckler and Koch, etc. With the range of "special ops" or "tactical" pistols on the market, there appears to be a sound, combat-proved firearm for nearly anyone's budget. Smith & Wesson offers, perhaps the widest selection economically and the better

---

[130] I *highly* recommend shopping at www.ammunitiontogo.com, www.luckygunner.com, and www.cheaperthandirt.com for a range of choices and fast, efficient service to your front door.

Model 1911 variants in .45 can run close to $1,000.[131] If you desire to do a lot of practice and do not wish to bother your neighbors, then you might want to choose a 1911 variant, such as those made by Sig-Sauer, with a threaded barrel for those locations that permit sound suppressors.

### *Assault Rifles*

With the expiration of the asinine "assault weapons" ban, Americans are now once again free to purchase firearms that are durable, adaptable, and reliable (much like newer cell phones and digital cameras). For the budget conscious, there remains a host of Kalashnikov rifles available, including AKM/AKMS (the modernized version of the AK-47 in semi-auto format, the 'S' designator representing a folding stock version, legally considered a "pistol") and the smaller 5.45x39mm caliber AK-74 as well as a range of actual pistol versions.[132] These American-made and/or imported rifles are easy to maintain and use and vast quantities of ammunition remain available for them through various retailers. While not as accurate at distances as the American AR style rifles, they remain sufficient for targets out to ~400 meters. Not to mention, your Islamist and narco terrorist enemies will almost exclusively use them. Therefore, at worst, you would be doing yourself a favor in understanding these firearms that have been notoriously vilified by the media and politicians.

For those with a bit more money to spend ($1000 to $3000+), there remains an entire industry of AR assault rifles in calibers ranging from the omnipresent 5.56mm on up through .50 Beowulf. My personal "urban rifle" remains a Ruger SR-556 in 6.8mm SPC (See figure 2). This round bears a bit more punch when shooting through, say, glass, than the

---

[131] Check www.impactguns.com, www.hyattgunstore.com, and www.knesekguns.com.
[132] See, for instance, www.atlanticfirearms.com.

easily splintered 5.56mm.

The beauty of the AR-15 variants remains their ability to accept accessories for the rifles with Picatinny rails installed on them. These include riflescopes, bipods, handgrips, red dot optics, reflex sights, lasers, night vision scopes, flashlights, even grenade launchers if you possess enough money. Spend your first dollar researching the *many* options available and then you may spend upwards of a year deciding on the best firearm for your particular situation.

**Figure 2. Author's "urbanized" Ruger SR-556 in 6.8 SPC.** Three-point tactical sling, 4x32 illuminated reticle mil-dot scope, bipod, and forward grip. © R.J. Godlewski

### Shotguns

A reliable .12 gauge shotgun loaded with 00 Buckshot remains the *best home defense weapon available* in my honest opinion. Just the sound of a pump being chocked in the darkness can terrify even the most hardcore intruder. A semi-auto shotgun can fling a virtual barrier of buckshot or slugs downrange without the need for an extra arm to rack a new round into the chamber.

As with all firearms, however, the availability of products evolves faster than any legitimate book can hope to discuss and this remains no different with shotguns. Winchester, Remington, and Mossberg represent just a few of the choices available and the uniqueness of the variety of ammunition makes the quality shotgun perhaps the best all-around firearm in existence. One gun can fire buckshot, slugs, tear gas, rubber bullets, flares, and even beanbags and breaching rounds to break down door hinges.

Remington's model 870 has been the military and police favorite for a great many years and their newer *887 NitroMag Tactical* offers a great option for those who fight the elements as well as assailants (not to mention states that outlaw pistol grips on long guns). Mossberg offers the best shotguns, perhaps, for those seeking to spend a little less money. One product, in particular, the *JIC* (Just in Case) *II* represents a "take down" version of the reliable Mossberg 500. Instead of the sealable tube that the other *JIC* models come in, the *JIC II* rests within a zippered nylon case that can attach to backpacks. The stockless, pistol-gripped shotgun is definitely *not* for recreational shooting, but can come in handy should you find yourself on the trail or bugging out after disaster strikes.

The entire shotgun *can* be assembled in less than 1-2 minutes, but *practice* remains advised as the procedure can escape one's attention rather quickly and, frankly, it serves little purpose to own the gun if you cannot assemble, load, and fire it before the threat reaches you. For most, I would recommend it as a gun that you would assemble once you reach your destination regardless of potential threats.

### Long Rifles

A long rifle for anything beyond hunting is probably not within your interests unless you cannot own handguns or purchase assault rifles where you live. A few diehards out there will probably seek to develop some form of personal sniper rifle and, well, go for it. For the uninitiated, a long rifle usually means that you are targeting beyond 300-400 meters and that means that you generally live outside the urban environment. For the rest of us mere mortals, there exists absolutely no reason to believe that we need high-powered, expensive rifles with even more expensive and powerful scopes for what amounts to "up close and personal" work dealing with urban terrorists.[133] My personal choice of the Ruger SR-556/6.8 SPC represents the maximum limit of practicality and exists for a fundamental – if somewhat personal – reason. As does my PTR-91 in .308 caliber (most people should purchase a proven battle rifle at some point to supplement their chosen assault rifle, particularly if you are actually considering the implications of this book).

Much can be done with standard hunting rifles as well as various military surplus rifles, such as the WWII-era Russian Mosin-Nagant (chambered in 7.62x54R) or the 1950s era Yugoslavian Mauser M-48 (firing an 8mm cartridge), both of which can be purchased in quantities in excellent shape for about $200 each. As these original words were being typed, the I-96 corridor in Southeastern Michigan – a few miles from here – had been hit at least 22 times by an unknown shooter engaging vehicular traffic.[134] From what I had seen of the damage to the cars, it appeared to be a larger caliber firearm, despite the police suspecting a handgun of some sort. Just a lesson in that threats can materialize from anywhere and from anyone...

Suitable, though more expensive, modern rifles include the PTR 91 series of H&K-inspired rifles in calibers ranging from 7.62x39mm to 7.62 NATO. The "paratrooper" version, which I own, the PTR-91 KFM4 makes for a fine urban battle rifle packing punch in a reduced size and yet offers three

---

[133] John West, *Fry the Brain: The Art of Urban Sniping and its Role in Modern Guerrilla Warfare* (Countryside, VA: SSI, 2008), 20-22.
[134] See http://www.nydailynews.com/news/national/i-96-mystery-sniper-strikes-wounded-article-1.1194140, accessed October 29, 2012.

Picatinny rails to support bipods, lights, etc.[135] It represents a sound and beautiful weapon to behold, but one existing at the outer limits of 'urban' range. After all, we *will* find ourselves on the periphery of cities from time to time.

## Infrastructure

The extraordinary rise of the Internet, smart phones, and high-speed wireless communications warrant inclusion into the 2014 edition of this book, though profound discussion must defer to other publications. It remains imperative, however, to mention that computer technology and the Internet represent two-edged swords. The volume of data that we expose to the outside world paralles the sheer amount of knowledge that can be discovered by the budding counterterrorist. Therefore, we shall begin with the *bad* side of the equation.

Do you possess a smartphone, Facebook account, post videos on YouTube, or spend more than twenty minutes of each hour on the cell phone? Then, friend, you have undoubtedly compromised your privacy (if not your integrity) *permanently.* Those *true* professionals – the kind whose associations prevent any humoring of "independent" status – avoid these technologies like the plague. In 2013, the world learned – to its bewilderment – that the U.S. National Security Agency spied upon American citizens. This was something that I heard about from a fellow classmate back in 2009 and, frankly, suspected as early as 1988.

The point remains whatever you hear upon the evening news rests at least four years old before the public gets wind of it. True, certain events appear during the same day, but they will likely take several years before the "facts" work their

---

[135] Visit www.PTR91.com.

way out. Nevertheless, you are going to have to work towards reducing your online presence. Totally disappearing is impossible since you have already managed to drop a great deal of knowledge for posterity. There can be no placing the genie back into the bottle. That said, *some* things can be done to provide you with a fair degree of protection.

The *first* thing that you should do remains to construct an 'infrastructure' away from your personal life – particularly if you possess a family or other business to protect. Begin by establishing a virtual office far away from your presence. Companies such as Opus Virtual Offices, Regus, and others provide receptionist, telephone, and mailing services within a great many of American (and foreign) cities. Through these business services, you can redirect mail, telephone calls, and even locations that adversaries will likely target in their search to find out information about you. Of course, any *true* adversary will likely know *where* you live, work, and shop but...

You will further need to build an infrastructure for training purposes. For example, you will need to train *extensively* with your firearms. Unfortunately, most public and private gun ranges are inadequate for your needs. Simply shooting paper targets with bull's-eyes is not very conducive to counterterrorist training. Actionable targets with *realistic* depictions of terrorists and other criminals are mandatory.[136] The more substantial your infrastructure, the more business-oriented your efforts will become.[137] Whatever route you choose to employ, *your* efforts must be solid and unforgiving for your enemies will *not* ignore your participation within their demise.

---

[136] See, for instance, www.letargets.com.
[137] See www.inertproducts.com.

# 9. REALITY CHECK 2014

**Figure 3. Independent Counterterrorist, European soldier, or pro-Russian/ anti-Ukrainian thug?** © Oleg Zabielin - Fotolia.com

There remains no more gruesome prospect to behold than the killing and maiming of another human being. The mere thought of a high-power bullet tearing through human flesh is more than most individuals can comprehend, which is why I intentionally truncated the weapons section beginning with the second, more distributed version of *Mini-Manual of the*

*Independent Counterterrorist*. However, if you are going to prepare for all "potentialities", including, specifically, shooting another human individual, than *you must fully understand* the implications of your or another's actions. Simply put, *never aim a firearm at another living soul unless you intend to kill them* and bear the legal, moral, and psychological implications of your action. Think of this as your "*Point a gun, go to jail; Use a gun, go to prison for life*" rule.

## Wound Ballistics

The primary property of a modern bullet in flight remains its velocity and its stability as affected by the spin imparted upon it from the rifling within the firearm's barrel. In this environment, the bullet rests within its realm and will carry on through its trajectory towards the ground under the auspices of gravity *unless* it impacts against an intruding target, wherein it either comes to an abrupt halt or ricochets.

When a bullet strikes human tissue – at roughly 800 to 900 times denser than air[138] – it immediately destabilizes and begins to tumble releasing its energy and causing injury in three ways (assuming that it did not represent a *powerful enough* bullet that it would pass through the body). The first represents the cutting and crushing of tissue as the bullet initially enters into the body. The second mechanism involves the shock wave produced by supersonic bullets; this travels outwards at the speed of sound within water – 4,800 feet per second.[139]

The third injury causing mechanism represents *temporary cavitation*. The bullet forces energy outward and *forward* when it enters the body, even producing momentum for long after the bullet has finally exited the victim. This

---

[138] Adrian Gilbert, *Sniper: One on One: The World of Combat Sniping* (London: Sidgwick & Jackson, 1994), 124.
[139] Ibid., 125.

energy release causes the formation of the large cavity that essentially consists of the wound track and may be upwards of *thirty times* the bullet diameter.[140] This effect remains so violent that it may destroy capillaries far removed from the actual path of the bullet.

Perhaps, it would behoove us to examine things from a different perspective. Let us take a less technical view of the 5.56mm AR-15 round. At distances of less than 100 yards, it is traveling at nearly three thousand feet per second when it strikes against the human body. The bullet, being small and unstable now, begins to tumble at, perhaps, ninety degrees before it reaches a full four inches into the body and begins to disintegrate into smaller fragments.[141] What had just been traveling at greater than the speed of sound – as if a military jet fighter on full afterburner – *stops* in a matter of a few inches. All that powerful momentum has to go *somewhere* and that somewhere represents the body's tissues, bones, and blood vessels.

What was once healthy living 'body' now remains a conduit for a supersonic shockwave traveling up virtually every blood vessel, through every cell, and reverberating within every fluid within your body. They literally explode until the energy is ultimately dissipated. I will spare you the rest, but just remember the effects of the slight "shock" of, say, your leg when it hits the ground a bit too hard. Now imagine that shock amplified thousands of times.

The human body is *not* rigid like a mannequin. It is mostly fluid with relatively few bones to keep the fluids and soft tissue into shape. What one part of your body experiences, the others share to a degree (we learned this through cross training). Therefore, a bullet hitting a human body (or animal body for that matter) does not simply "drill" a

---

[140] Ibid., 126.
[141] Ibid., 129.

hole through a solid object. It *pierces a fluid object* and the resulting shock waves literally vaporize anything that is not solid. Should this "fluid object" represent, say, the human brain, then the resulting damage magnifies exponentially as untold millions of electrical impulses shoot throughout the body *instantaneously*. Chickens are *not* the only animals that can briefly scurry around without heads attached.

### Shot in Self Defense

You have just been involved within a shooting at a local shopping mall, what do you *do*? First *you* have to call the 911 operator and report the incident – *do not trust anyone else on this matter!* Tell the operator your full name and *complete description*. Describe the incident to the utmost detail without – insofar as possible – addressing your shooting of the aggressor (do mention that the shooter has not fled the site but there is no danger remaining). Do *not* say that some ugly ass white guy accosted your wife and therefore you blew his head off. Describe the aggressor's clothing in detail (e.g., white sleeveless tee shirt, tan trousers, New York Yankees jacket, etc.) as well as your own. *Tell the operator that you will remain there until the police arrive.*

When the police do arrive, do not announce yourself as the shooter but place your gun down slowly and calmly upon the floor, and state that you bear a concealed carry permit for defense, and then do *exactly* as they tell you without adding any further comments. You will likely be escorted down to the station to make a statement but do not make *any* statements. Follow the advice provided by a former federal attorney:

> "No matter who you are, no matter how smart you are, if you are confronted by Law Enforcement, assert your rights by saying:
> "You WILL have my full COOPERATION within 24

hours. I WANT to speak with my ATTORNEY. I will NOT answer any QUESTIONS. I will NOT make a STATEMENT at this time. You may NOT SEARCH my vehicle, home, or property. Am I free to LEAVE? I want to leave NOW.

"BE POLITE AND RESPECTFUL TO THE POLICE. NEVER PHYSICALLY RESIST THE POLICE."[142]

The local DA may not particularly like your self-preservation efforts; so long before you even come near to getting into such trouble, do *not* include hand reloads in your gun or else they may consider you as being "pre-meditated" for hand loading your ammunition specifically "for the crime". Furthermore, if you bear *any* military background, most states already conclude that you are a trained killer despite what that military background actually entails. God forbid, please *do not* carry this book around with you. Lastly, if the mall people attempt to sue you for bringing a gun into their "gun-free" establishment, go ahead and counter-sue for not protecting your life in the first place. In short, however, expect treatment by all as if a criminal and have your life disrupted for years – if not forever. At least you will *still* be alive.

### Some Final Lessons

"*War is cruelty, and you cannot refine it.*"
Gen. William Tecumseh Sherman
"*In the end, we simply cut and ran. The American national will had collapsed...*"
Graham A. Martin, former U.S. Ambassador to South Vietnam"
"*One committed to dying can be slain.*"
Sun-tzu

Yours is going to become a very lonely life. It just

---

[142] Courtesy Law Office of John Freeman, Troy, Michigan. Information pulled from the back of attorney business card. www.formerfedlawyer.com.

cannot be helped. You will find yourself tucked up against a wall of resentment no matter where you go. On the one hand, you will have the terrorists and their sympathizers. Those you can probably deal with because they represent largely known qualities. On the other hand, however, you will find yourself confronted with people who will take exception to what you are doing. Amongst these are the *perennial complainers* ("It's all the government's fault"; "Blame the wealthy", etc.); the *confused* ("Listen, I work in a school and the police told *me* exactly what to do, therefore I know a thing or two about terrorism", etc.); and, of course, the *Anti-Religion/Wrong Religion* crowd ("I do not believe in all of these "High and Mighty' people, they are just a bunch of hypocrites!" or, conversely, "You're maligning the Muslims unfairly!").

You have dealt with these people all of your life. They represent the ones who will, for instance, drive a Ford pickup truck and inform you of every single Chevrolet they have seen broken down along the highway or vice versa. They represent the kind of people who *will not* vote simply because their particular candidate was bumped out during the primaries. Worse, still, are the ones who profoundly believe in Bigfoot, UFOs, and "professional" wrestling but will not admit to it being a form of religion on their part.

They will deny *your* opinion because they cannot believe how *anyone* could ignore *their* evidence. You might see a mangy bear scratching himself against a tree instead of a Sasquatch or a particularly bright manifestation of the planet Venus instead of a spaceship from Rigel 7, but that does not appear to faze them because "it all represents a great big government cover-up". You cannot do anything with these people, so you will just end up ignoring them for the long haul.

As I said, yours is going to represent a *very lonely* life. You will find yourself spending more and more time *researching* than *entertaining*. You will notice that when you read, you read military and historical texts. When you watch television, you are probably glued to *Fox News* or the *American Heroes Channel*. When you receive your tax refund check, you are not thinking about getting new tires for your car or finally calling the plumber to fix that leaky sink, you are thinking about how much more ammo you can purchase so that you can practice just a little bit more.

They have always said that it remains lonely at the *top*, but you will be wading through the putrid bottom. Any spare time that you can extract from your "necessities" will be worked into your already strained counterterrorism schedule. You have much research to do, many supplies to order, and technology to inquire about. While information technology may have never represented your forte – too many concentrate on securing the networks to the exclusion of taking the fight to the terrorists – you are still interested in setting up a grid-computing network within your home.[143] You will want to turn all those PCs, tablets, and laptops within your home into a 'poor man's supercomputer' for analyzing threats and assimilating Geospatial Intelligence."

Yet, what makes you feel lonely is perhaps the knowledge that few people – even those who once purported to have understood the Global War on Terror – believe that the Islamists or the narco traffickers remain as much a threat as you know them to be. You have come across some compatriots, but they just did not quite pan out. You found that they usually belonged to one of the foregoing groups of people. They, for instance, wanted to use their guns for mayhem or some other ridiculous task. You may have found yourself mumbling, "I am *not* forming some form of 'Redneck Army' here – I am a professional!" And right you *are.*

Others from the "government knows best" crowd, who blindly venture through life believing that they are always

---

[143] Ahmar Abbas, *Grid Computing: A Practical Guide to Technology and Applications* (Hingham, MA: Charles River Media, 2004), 32-41.

protected, will think ill of you. These represent the people who do not wear seatbelts because airbags will protect them from injury. Had they ever bothered to watch videos of crash test dummies having their heads thrown through the rear windows, they would understand that seatbelts are required *particularly* with airbags. Local bureaucrats who believe you to represent some form of innate threat to the observable universe remain far too numerous to reflect upon here.

This may appear to represent a very depressing way of life besides one that remains inherently lonely, but it really is not. I find immense joy and satisfaction, not to mention a strong sense of duty in what I do and for which I remain confident has attracted you to combating terrorism in your own little way too. There is a strong sense of pride (patriotic and otherwise) in knowing that you must keep on your toes every minute of every day for decades on end. That you must examine, too, every little facet of your life and habits for necessary reforms and rehabilitation.

While others continually purchase lottery tickets because "Sooner or later, I will be lucky!", you practice and prepare for survival because, sooner or later, you will definitely *not* be so lucky. You simply cannot accept chances with your life. Your team loses because they failed to prepare, *not* because the referees were screwy or the weather was against them, or there were too many injuries. You expect bad things to happen and pray daily that God keeps them to a minimum – not expect good things and only pray to God when the truly horrible arrives. You use the tools that He gave to you to continue living because you understand that the "other guy" may be praying too and God generally does not play favorites.

Yes, your life will indeed become lonely, but very exciting – just like the astronomer of old who sat high up in his mountaintop observatory consciously observing the night sky. He did not seek fame or fortune. He did it simply to understand the sheer beauty and complexity of the world before him. He could see the threats out there – threats that could, someday, literally extinguish the human race – but he also knew that he might not be around when they came into play. His work existed just so that humanity *could* survive from his efforts…

## Addendum

Since the first two editions of this particular book, the world has continued to descend into the seeming omnipresence of evil. Certainly, humanity has left much to desire owing to the continuing exploits of Russia, China, Iran, Syria, North Korea, Egypt, and other decidedly non-democratic nations. What we see upon the television news or read casually on the Internet is probably *not* the facts.

Do you believe, for a moment, that a President of the United States remains the most powerful figure in the world? Not with our current stable of secret service agents. True, some may say that these "protectors" of the president bear a fundamental right to party during the off hours but, sadly, terrorists and transnational criminals do *not* possess an off button. Who could be safe with protection *half* the time? In fact, if someone *were* to attack a sitting president, do you really believe that they will cut straight for the jugular so to speak? Hardly.

Personally, I would begin to worry when the media begins to report a series of attacks against family members of the U.S. Secret Service. *Then* you will realize that something terrible is going to happen. It takes a determined and *disciplined* individual to safeguard another when his or her own family is systematically being murdered. Terrorists and transnational criminals are *not* human, but we expect our military and security personnel to be *fully* human. And they are.

Societal breakdowns happen within every aspect of

human community – not just major urban centers or entire nations. When you read stories of secret service agents carousing with prostitutes or partying in bars "after hours", how does that make *you* feel? Would *you* want such people protecting your life if you were serving as president? Probably not, for we all remain a bit self-centered at heart. Nevertheless, U.S. Secret Service personnel are reputed to be the literal best of the best for the simple role that they provide.

Unfortunately, if "the best" is not good enough for our national leaders, how much more so can *your* personal protection hope to be? Again, unless your life represents the pantheon of global power, *others* will not view you as valuable or your family's life as worthy of service. You represent your family's first, future, and last line of defense. Now, how good are you *really*? Time is literally running out if for no other reason than you bear finite days here upon earth. Fortunately, you still have a future if you change during this second. Otherwise, the end will likely come when you least expect it.

Imagine yourself mysteriously cast out upon the surface of an uninhabited alien planet deep in the recesses of the universe. Confronting you appears another strange being, one whose mannerisms and beliefs remain diametrically opposed to *everything* you stand for. To make matters far more difficult, you have to actively *search* for food, water, and shelter but the other being simply knows that you stand in his way towards the same resources. What do *you* do?

************

# CONSULTED LITERATURE

Abbas, Ahmar. *Grid Computing: A Practical Guide to Technology and Applications.* Hingham, MA: Charles River Media, Inc., 2004.

AbuKhalil, As'ad. "Arab-Israeli Conflict." In *The Middle East*, by CQ Press, 13-78. Washington: CQ Press, 2005.

Akhavan, Jacqueline. *The Chemistry of Explosives.* Second Edition. Cambridge: Royal Society of Chemistry, 2006.

Allison, Graham. *Nuclear Terrorism: The Ultimate Preventable Catastrophe.* New York: Times Books, 2004.

Aloise, Gene, interview by the Federal Workforce, and the District of Columbia, Committee on Homeland Security and Governmental Affairs, U.S. Senate Subcommittee on Oversight of Government Management. *COMBATING NUCLEAR TERRORISM: Federal Efforts to Respond to Nuclear and Radiological Threats and to Protect Key Emergency Response Facilities Could Be Strengthened.* U.S. Government Accountability Office, (November 15, 2007).

al-Qaeda. "Declaration of Jihad (Holy War) Against the Country's Tyrants, Military Series."

Alterman, Jon B. *The Real Shi'a-Sunni Conflict.* Washington: Center for Strategic and International Studies, 2007.

Andrew, Christopher, and Vasili Mitrokhin. *The Sword and the Shield: The Mitrokhin Archive and the Secret History of the KGB.* New York: Basic Books, 1999.

Argonne National Laboratory. *Radiological Disperal Device (RDD).* Human Health Fact Sheet, Chicago: Argonne National Laboratory, 2005.

Arias, Enrique Desmond. "Understanding Criminal Networks, Political Order, and Politics in Latin America." In *Ungoverned Spaces: Alternatives to State Authority in an Era of Softened Sovereignty*, edited by Anne L. Clunan and Harold A. Trinkunas, 115-135. Stanford, CA: Stanford Security Studies/Stanford University Press, 2010.

Armstrong, Karen. *A History of God: The 4,000-Year Quest of Judaism, Christianity, and Islam.* New York: Ballantine Books, 1993.

Aslan, Reza. *No god but God: The Origins, Evolution, and Future of Islam.* New York: Random House, 2006.

Baer, Robert. "Politics: GQ." *GQ Magazine Web site.* April 2010. http://www.gq.com/news-politics/politics/201004/dagger-to-the-cia (accessed April 17, 2010).

—. *See No Evil: The True Story of a Ground Soldier in the CIA's War on Terrorism.* New York: Three Rivers Press, 2002.

Balor, Paul. *Manual of the Mercenary Soldier.* Boulder: Paladin Press, 1988.

Beason, Doug. *The E-Bomb: How America's New Directed Energy Weapons Will Change the Way Future Wars Will Be Fought.* Cambridge, MA: Da Capo Press, 2005.

Beevor, Antony. *Stalingrad: The Fateful Siege: 1942-1943.* New York: Penguin Books, 1998.

Bejtlich, Richard. "Cooking the Cuckoo's Egg." Vers. 1.0. *Tao Security Website.* February 2, 2011. http://www.taosecurity.com/bejtlich_doj_cooking_06feb11a.pdf (accessed December 13, 2012).

Bennett, Matthew, Jim Bradbury, Kelly DeVries, Iain Dickie, and Phyllis Jestice. *Fighting Techniques of the Medieval World.* New York: Thomas Dunne Books, 2005.

Benson, Ragnar. *Gunrunning for Fun & Profit.* Boulder: Paladin Press, 1986.

Bergman, Ronen. "Hezbollah and the Lebanon Dilemma." *Wall Street Journal (Eastern edition)*, August 5, 2010: A17.

Biddle, Stephen, and Jeffrey A. Friedman. *THE 2006 LEBANON CAMPAIGN AND THE FUTURE OF WARFARE: Implications for Army and Defense Policy.* Carlisle, PA: Strategic Studies Institute, 2008.

Black, Ian, and Benny Morris. *Israel's Secret Wars: A History of Israel's Intelligence Services.* New York: Grove Press, 1991.

Blandford, Edmund L. *SS Intelligence.* Shrewsbury: Airlife Publishing Ltd., 2000.

Bodansky, Yossef. *Chechen Jihad: Al-Qaeda's Training Ground and the Next Wave of Terror.* New York: Harper, 2007.

—. "CHECHNYA: The Mujahedin Factor."

—. *TERROR! The inside story of the terrorist conspiracy in America.* SPI Books, 1994.

Bowden, Mark. *Killing Pablo: The Hunt for the World's Greatest Outlaw.* New York: Penguin Books, 2001.

Brands, Hal. *Crime, Violence, and the Crisis in Guatemala: A Case Study in the Erosion of the State.* Strategic Study, Carlisle: Strategic Studies Institute, 2010.

Brands, Hal. *Mexico's Narco-Insurgency and U.S. Counterdrug Policy.* Strategic Study, Carlisle, PA: Strategic Studies Institute, 2009.

Braun, Martin. *Differential Equations and Their Applications.* Fourth Edition. New York: Springer-Verlag, 1993.

Byman, Daniel. *Deadly Connections: States that Sponsor Terrorism.* New York: Cambridge University Press, 2005.

Celeski, Joseph D. *Hunter-Killer Teams: Attacking Enemy Safe Havens.* Report 10-1, Hurlburt Field, FL: Joint Special Operations University, 2010.

Chambers, Larry. *RECONDO: LRRPs in the 101st Airborne.* New York: Ballantine Books, 1992.

Chinn, Ko-lin. *Chinatown Gangs: Extortion, Enterprise, & Ethnicity.* New York: Oxford University Press, 1996.

Clark, Robert M. *Intelligence Analysis: A target-centric approach.* Washington: CQ Press, 2007.

Clarke, Richard A., and Robert K. Knake. *Cyber War: The Next Threat to National Security and What to Do about It.* New York: Harper Collins/Ecco, 2010.

Clausewitz, Carl von. *On War.* Translated by Michael Howard and Peter Paret. Princeton: Princeton University Press, 1984.

Coll, Steve. *Ghost Wars: The Secret History of the CIA, Afghanistan, and Bin Laden, from the Soviet Invasion to Steptember 10, 2001.* New York: Penguin Books, 2004.

Cooper, Andy. "Training for a Mission in an IED Threat Environment." *MilitaryTechnology*, December 2008: 68-68.

Couch, Dick. *A Tactical Ethic: Moral Conduct in the Insurgent Battlespace.* Annapolis, MD: Naval Institute Press, 2010.

Cox, Robert. "Total Terrorism: Argentina, 1969 to 1979." In *Terrorism, Legitimacy, and Power*, by Martha Crenshaw, 124-142. Middletown, CT: Wesleyan, 1983.

Cragin, Kim, and Bruce Hoffman. *Arms Trafficking and Colombia.* Santa Monica, CA: RAND Corporation, 2003.

Crawford, George A. *Manhunting: Counter-Network Organization for Irregular Warfare.* JSOU Report 09-7, Hurlbert Field: Joint Special Operations University, 2009.

Crawford, Steve. *Deadly Fighting Skills of the World.* London: Brown Books, 1997.

Cross, Michael. *Scene of the Cybercrime.* Second. Burlington, MA: Syngress Publishing, 2008.

Cwiek, Mark A. *America after 9/11.* Vol. I, chap. 2 in *Community Preparedness and Response to Terrorism: The Terrorist Threat and Community Response*, edited by Gerald R. Ledlow, James A. Johnson and Walter J. Jones, 7-21. Westport, Connecticut: Praeger, 2005.

Dashti, Ali. "Twenty Three Years: A study of the Prophetic Career of Mohammad." 1994.

Dauber, Cori I. *YouTube War: Fighting in a World of Cameras in every Cell Phone and Photoshop on every Computer.* Carlisle, PA: Strategic Studies Institute, 2009.

Daugherty, William J. "Approval and Review of Covert Action Programs Since Reagan." *International Journal of Intelligence*, 2004: 62-80.

de Wijze, Stephen. "Targeted killing: a 'dirty hands' analysis." *Contemporary Politics* 15, no. 3 (September 2009): 305-320.

Decker, Scott H., and Margaret Townsend Chapman. *Drug Smugglers on Drug Smuggling: Lessons from the Inside.* Philadelphia: Temple University Press, 2008.

Department of the Army. *FM 3-05.30 PSYCHOLOGICAL OPERATIONS.* Field Manual, Washington: United States Government, 2005.

Department of the Army, Headquarters. *FM 3-55.93 Long-Range Surveillance Unit Operations.* Washington: United States Government, 2009.

Dobson, Christopher, and Ronald Payne. *Counterattack: The West's battle against the terrorists.* New York: Facts on File, Inc., 1982.

Donnelly, Tom. "A Question of Faith: Conflicts Driven by Religion Can be Long and Bitter." *Armed Forces Journal*, October 2006: 60-62.

Durant, Will. *The Age of Faith.* New York: Simon and Schuster, 1950.

Ehrenfeld, Rachel. *Funding Evil: How Terrorism is Financed -- and How to Stop it.* Chicago: Bonus Books, 2003.

Elaasar, Aladdin. "Is Egypt Stable?" *Middle East Quarterly*, 2009: 69-75.

Ellis, John W. *Police Analysis and Planning for Homicide Bombings: Prevention, Defense, and Response.* Springfield, IL: Charles C. Thomas Publisher, Ltd., 2007.

Emerson, Steven. *American Jihad: The Terrorists Living Amongst Us.* New York: The Free Press, 2002.

England, James W. *Long-Range Patrol Operations: Reconnaissance, Combat, and Special Operations.* Boulder: Paladin Press, 1987.

Eshel, David. "Defeating IEDs." *The Journal of Electronic Defense*, December 2007: 38-42.

Fainaru, Steve. *Big Boy Rules: America's Mercenaries Fighting in Iraq.* Philadelphia: Da Capo Press, 2008.

Fay, John J. *Contemporary security management.* Third. Burlington, MA: Buttersworth-Heinemann, 2011.

Felbab-Brown, Vanda. *The Violent Drug Market in Mexico and Lessons from Colombia.* Foreign Policy Study, Washington: Brookings Institute, 2009.

Ferguson, Charles D., and William C. Potter. *Improvised Nuclear Devices and Nuclear Terrorism.* Research Paper, Stockholm: The Weapons of Mass Destruction Commission, 2004.

Fishel, John T., and Max G. Manwaring. *Uncomfortable Wars Revisited.* Norman, OK: University of Oklahoma Press, 2006.

Flanigan, Shawn Teresa, and Mounah Abdel-Samad. "Hezbollah's Social Jihad: Nonprofits as Resistance Organizations." *Middle East Policy* XVI, no. 2 (2009): 122-137.

Fowler, Will. *The Special Forces Guide to Escape and Evasion.* New York: Thomas Dunne Books, 2005.

Frey, Bruno S. *Why Kill Politicians? A Rational Choice Analysis of Political Assassinations.* Working Paper, Basel: Center for Research in Economics, Management and the Arts, 2007.

Gabriel, Mark A. *Journey into the Mind of an Islamic Terrorist.* Lake Mary, Florida: Front Line, 2006.

Gander, Terry. *Guerrilla Warfare Weapons: The Modern Underground Fighter's Armoury.* New York: Sterling Publishing Co., Inc., 1990.

Garner, Robert J. *Ethical Guidelines for Military Covert Operations.* USAWC Military Studies Program Paper, Carlisle Barracks, Pennsylvania: U.S. Army War College, 1990.

Gerges, Fawaz. *Journey of the Jihadist: Inside Muslim Militancy.* Orlando: Harcourt, 2006.

Glazebrook, Jerry, and Nick Nicholson. *Executive Protection Specialist Handbook.* Second Edition. Shawnee Mission, Kansas: Varro Press, 2003.

Godlewski, R.J. "Cultivating Creativity within Intelligence Analysis." *American Intelligence Journal* 25, no. 2 (2008): 85-87.

Godlewski, R.J. "Financial Counterintelligence: Fractioning the Lifeblood of Asymmetrical Warfare." *American Intelligence Journal* 29, no. 2 (2011): 24-33.

Godlewski, R.J. "Human Intelligence: Perceiving an Enemy's Thoughts." *American Intelligence Journal* 27, no. 1 (2009): 29-37.

Godlewski, R.J. "Latte Intelligence: The Divorce of Shock Creativity and Special Information Operations." *American Intelligence Journal* 29, no. 1 (2011): 70-79.

—. *Mini-Manual of the Independent Counterterrorist.* Second. Charleston, SC: CreateSpace Independent Publishing Platform, 2012.

—. *Skills of the Assassin: Understanding the Tactics of the Professional Killer.* Charleston: CreateSpace Independent Publishing Platform, 2012.

Goodman, Martin. *Rome and Jerusalem: The Clash of Ancient Civilizations.* New York: Alfred A. Knopf, 2007.

Goodrich, Thomas. *Scalp Dance: Indian Warfare on the High Plains 1865-1879.* Mechanicsburg , Pennsylvania: Stackpole Books, 1997.

Gourevitch, Philip. *We wish to inform you that tomorrow we will be killed with our families.* New York: Picador, 1998.

Gray, Colin S. *Another Bloody Century: Future Warfare.* London: Phoenix, 2006.

Gray, Jim, Mark Monday, and Gary Stubblefield. *Maritime Terror: Protecting Yourself, Your Vessel, and Your Crew against Piracy.* Boulder: Paladin Press, 2011.

Grayson, George W. *La Familia Drug Cartel: Implications for U.S.-Mexican Security.* Carlisle, PA: Strategic Studies Institute, 2010.

—. *Threat Posed by Mounting Vigilantism in Mexico.* Carlisle, PA: Strategic Studies Institute, 2011.

Gross, Michael L. *Moral Dilemmas of Modern War: Torture, Assassination, and Blackmail in an Age of Asymmetric Conflict.* New York: Cambridge University Press, 2010.

Grossman, Dave. *On Killing: The Psychological Cost of Learning to Kill in War and Society.* Revised. New York: Back Bay Books, 2009.

Grossman, David A. "Defeating the Enemy's Will: The Psychological Foundations of Maneuver Warfare." In *Maneuver Warfare: An Anthology*, by Jr. ed. Richard D. Hooker. Novato, CA: Presidio Press, 1993.

Guevara, Che. *Guerrilla Warfare.* New York: Monthly Review Press, 1961.

Hadley, Arthur T. "Maneuver Warfare and the Art of Deception." In *Maneuver Warfare: An Anthology*, by Richard D. (Ed) Hooker. Novato, CA: Presidio Press, 1993.

Hamilton, Scott. "Cyber Threats: We don't know what we don't know." *Armed Forces Journal*, November 2009: 33-34, 41.

Harclerode, Peter. *Fighting Dirty: The Inside Story of Covert Operations from Ho Chi Minh to Osama Bin Laden.* London: Cassell & Company, 2001.

Harold A. Winters with Gerald E. Galloway, Jr., William J. Reynolds, & David W. Rhyne. *Battling the Elements: Weather and terrain in the conduct of war.* Baltimore: Johns Hopkins University Press, 1998.

Hauner, Milan. "Terrorism and Heroism: The Assassination of Reinhard Heydrich." *World Policy Journal*, Summer 2007: 85-89.

Hayes, Stephen K. *The Ninja and their secret fighting art.* Rutland, VT: Charles E. Tuttle Company, 1981.

Headquarters, Department of the Army. *FM 3-06 Combined Arms Operations in Urban Terrain.* Washington: Department of the Army, 2002.

Heiden, Konrad. *Der Fuehrer: Hitler's rise to power.* Boston: Houghton Mifflin Company, 1944.

Herrington, Stuart A. *Stalking the Vietcong: Inside Operation Phoenix: A Personal Account.* New York: Ballantine Books, 1982.

Herzog, Chaim. *The Arab-Israeli Wars: War and Peace in the Middle East from the War of Independence through Lebanon.* New York: Vintage, 1982.

Heuer Jr., Richards J., and Randolph H. Pherson. *Structured Analytic Techniques For Intelligence Analysis.* Washington: CQ Press, 2011.

Hoffman, Bruce. "A Nasty Business." In *Terrorism and Counterterrorism: Understanding the New Security Environment: Readings and Interpretations*, by Russell D. Howard and Reid L. Sawyer, 402-407. Dubuque, Iowa: McGraw-Hill, 2006.

Hoffman, Frank G. "Mind Maneuvers: The Psychological Element of Counterinsurgency Warfare can be the Most Persuasive." *Armed Forces Journal*, April 2007: 28-32.

Holder, Philip T., and Donna Lea Hawley. *The Executive Protection Professional's Manual.* Boston: Butterworth-Heinemann, 1998.

Hristov, Jasmin. "Self-Defense Forces, Warlords, or Criminal Gangs? Towards a New Conceptualization of Paramilitarism in Colombia." *Labour, Capital & Society* 43, no. 2 (2010): 14-56.

Hunter, Thomas B. *Targeted Killing: Self-Defense, Preemption, and the War on Terrorism.* Lexington, KY: BookSurge, 2009.

Hurth, John D. *Combat Tracking Guide.* Mechanicsburg, PA: Stackpole Books, 2012.

Jaber, Hala. *Hezbollah: Born with a Vengeance.* New York: Columbia University Press, 1997.

Joes, Anthony James. *Urban Guerrilla Warfare.* Lexington: University Press of Kentucky, 2007.

Johnson, William R. *Thwarting Enemies at Home and Abroad: How to be a Counterintelligence Officer.* Washington: Georgetown University Press, 2009.

Jomini, Antoine-Henri. *The Art of War.* Translated by G.H. Mendell and W.P. Craighill. Rockville, MD: Arc Manor, 2007.

Jones, Adam. "Parainstitutional Violence in Latin America." *Latin American Politics and Society* 46, no. 4 (2004): 127-148.

Jones, Andy, Gerald I Kovacich, and Perry G. Luzwick. *Global Information Warfare: How Businesses, Governments, and Others Achieve Objectives and Attain Competitive Advantages.* New York: Auerbach, 2002.

Jones, Ishmael. *The Human Factor: Inside the CIA's Dysfunctional Intelligence Culture.* New York: Encounter Books, 2010.

Jonsson, Fredrik C. *Maritime Sniper Manual: Precision Fire from Seaborne Platforms.* Boulder: Paladin Press, 2010.

Kagan, Donald. *The Peloponnesian War.* New York: Viking, 2003.

Kahaner, Larry. *AK-47: The weapon that changed the face of war.* Hoboken: John Wiley & Sons, Inc., 2007.

Kahn, David. *Hitler's Spies: German Military Intelligence in World War II.* New York: Collier Books, 1978.

Kan, Paul Rexton. *Drug Intoxicated Irregular Fighters: Complications, Dangers, and Responses.* Carlisle, PA: Strategic Studies Institute, 2008.

—. *Mexico's "Narco-Refugees": The Looming Challenge for U.S. National Security.* Carlisle, PA: Strategic Studies Institute, 2011.

Kay, Christobal. "Reflections on Rual Violence in Latin America." *Third World Quarterly* 22, no. 5 (2001): 741-775.

Kellner, Tomas, and Francesco Pipitone. "Inside Mexico's Drug War." *World Policy Journal*, 2010: 29-37.

Kenney, Michael. *From Pablo to Osama: Trafficking and Terrorist Networks, Government Bureaucracies, and Competitive Adaptation.* University Park, PA: The Pennsylvania State University Press, 2007.

Kenney, Michael. "The Architecture of Drug Trafficking: Network Forms of Organisation in the Colombian Cocaine Trade." *Global Crime* 8, no. 3 (2007): 233-259.

Kennison, Peter, and Amanda Loumansky. "Shoot to kill -- understanding police use of force in combatting suicide terrorism." *Crime, Law, and Social Change* 47, no. 3 (2007): 151-168.

Kiernan, Kathleen L. "Counterintelligence and Law Enforcement." In *Vaults, Mirrors, & Masks: Rediscovering U.S. Counterintelligence*, by Jennifer E. Sims and Burton Gerber, 149-171. Washington: Georgetown University Press, 2009.

Klein, Aaron J. *Striking Back: The 1972 Munich Olympics Massacre and Israel's Deadly Response.* New York: Random House, 2007.

Knott, Stephen F. *Secret and Sanctioned: Covert operations and the American presidency.* New York: Oxford University Press, 1996.

Koch, Oscar W. with Robert G. Hayes. *G-2: Intelligence for Patton.* Atglen: Schiffer Military History, 1999.

Kouzminov, Alexander. *Biological Espionage: Special Operations of the Soviet and Russian Foreign Intelligence Services in the West.* London: Greenhill Books, 2005.

Kovats-Bernat, J. Christopher. "Factional Terror, Paramilitarism and Civil War in Haiti: The View from Port-au-Prince, 1994-2004." *Anthropologia* 48 (2006): 117-139.

Kreeft, Peter. *Everything you ever wanted to know about Heaven but never dreamed of asking!* San Francisco: Ignatius, 1990.

Kushner, Harvey, and Bart Davis. *Holy War on the Home Front: The Secret Islamic Terror Network in the United States.* New York: Sentinel, 2004.

Lambakis, Steven J. "Reconsidering Asymmetric Warfare." *Joint Force Quarterly*, 2004: 102-108.

Lanning, Michael Lee. *Inside the LRRPs: Rangers in Vietnam.* New York: Presidio Press, 2006.

Laqueur, Walter. *The Age of Terrorism.* Boston: Little, Brown and Company, 1987.

Lawrence, Erik. *Tactical Pistol Shooting.* Iola, WI: Gun Digest Books, 2005.

Lawrence, T.E. *Seven Pillars of Wisdom.* New York: Doubleday, Doran & Company, Inc., 1935.

Lee, Gregory D. *Global Drug Enforcement: Practical Investigative Techniques.* Boca Raton, FL: CRC Press, 2004.

Leebaert, Derek. *To Dare and to Conquer: Special Operations and the Destiny of Nations from Achilles to Al Qaeda.* New York: Back Bay Books, 2006.

Lichetenwald, Terrance G., Mara H. Steinhour, and Frank S. Perri. "A Maritime Threat Assessment of Sea Based Criminal Organizations and Terrorist Operations." *Homeland Security Affairs* 8, no. 13 (August 2012): 1-24.

Lind, Wiliam S., Keith Nightengale, John F. Schmitt, Joseph W. Sutton, and Gary I. Wilson. "The Changing Face of War: Into the Fourth Generation." In *Global Insurgency and the Future of Armed Conflict*, edited by Terry Terriff, Karp, Aaron and Regina Karp, 13-20. New York: Routledge, 2008.

Lung, HaHa. *Assassin! The Deadly Art of the Cult of the Assassins.* New York: Citadel Press, 1997.

Lung, Haha. *Mind Control: The Ancient Art of Psychological Warfare.* New York: Citadel Press, 2006.

Machiavelli, Niccolo. *The Prince.* Translated by Luigi Ricci. London: Grant Richards, 1903.

Machine, Garret. *Israeli Security Warrior Training.* Boulder: Paladin Press, 2011.

Mack, Jefferson. *Running a Ring of Spies: Spycraft and Black Operations in the Real World of Espionage.* Boulder: Paladin Press, 1996.

Magee, Aden C. "Counterintelligence in Irregular Warfare: A Void in the Full-Spectrum Joint Force Capability." *American Intelligence Journal*, Winter 2009: 54-60.

Manwaring, Max G. *A "New" Dynamic in the Western Hemisphere Security Environment: The Mexican Zetas and Other Private Armies.* Security Study, Carlisle: Strategic Studies Institute, 2009.

Manwaring, Max G. *State and Nonstate Associated Gangs: Credible "Midwives of New Social Orders".* Strategic Study, Carlisle: Strategic Studies Institute, 2009.

Marcella, Gabriel. *War without Borders: The Colombia-Ecuador Crisis of 2008.* Strategic Study, Carlisle, PA: Strategic Studies Institute, 2008.

Marighella, Carlos. *Mini-Manual of the Urban Guerrilla.*

Marks, Thomas A. "A Model Counterinsurgency: Uribe's Colombia (2002-2006) vs FARC." *Military Review*, March-April 2007: 41-56.

Martines, Larry. "Mexican Crime Cartels." *Journal of Counterterrorism & Homeland Security International* 18, no. 1 (2012): 36-40.

May, Timothy. *THE MONGOL ART OF WAR: Chinggis Khan and the Mongol Military System.* Book Club. Yardley, PA: Westholme Publishing, 2007.

McLaughlin, Abraham. *A matter of ethics for cloak-and-dagger set.* October 5, 2001. http://www.csmonitor.com/2001/1005/p2s1-usju.html (accessed July 23, 2010).

McMains, Michael J, and Wayman C. Mullins. *Crisis Negotiations: Managing Critical Incidents and Hostage Situations in Law Enforcement and Corrections.* 4th. New Providence, NJ: Matthew Bender & Company, 2010.

McNicholas, Michael. *Maritime Security: An Introduction.* Burlington, MA: Elsevier, 2008.

McRaven, William H. *SPEC OPS: Case Studies in Special Operations Warfare: Theory and Practice.* New York: Ballantine Books, 1996.

Melton, H. Keith, and Robert Wallace. *The Official C.I.A. Manual of Trickery and Deception.* New York: William Morrow, 2009.

Mendell, Ronald L. *The Quiet Threat: Fighting Industrial Espionage in America.* Second. Springfield, IL: Charles C. Thomas Publisher, 2011.

Merari, Ariel. "The readiness to kill and die: Suicidal terrorism in the Middle East." In *Origins of Terrorism: Psychologies, Ideologies, Theologies, States of Mind*, by Walter Reich, 192-207. Washington: Woodrow Wilson Center Press, 1998.

Miller, Colin R. *Electromagnetic Pulse Threats in 2010.* Threat Analysis, Maxwell AFB: Center for Strategy and Technology, Air War College/Air University, 2005.

Milton-Edwards, Beverley. *Contemporary Politics in the Middle East.* Second Edition. Cambridge: Polity, 2006.

Minieri, Michael W. *Protecting Corporate Secrets: A Brief Primer on Contemporary Practices in Information Security.* White Paper, Reston: Kroll Schiff & Associates, 2004.

Morris, Benny. *Israel's Border Wars 1949-1956.* New York: Oxford University Press, Inc., 1997.

Murphy, Martin, N. *Small Boats, Weak States, Dirty Money: Piracy and Maritime Terrorism in the Modern World.* New York: Columbia University Press, 2010.

Musashi, Miyamoto. "The Book of Five Rings." 1645.

Nasheri, Hedieh. *Economic Espionage and Industrial Spying.* New York: Cambridge University Press, 2005.

Nordmann, Brian D. "The Tyranny of Experts: Analytical Misperception and the Rise of State-Run Biological Weapons Programs." *Dissertation.* Fairfax, Virginia: George Mason University, 2008.

Norell, James O.E. "Are you an American or Are you a Terrorist?" *America's 1st Freedom*, September: 30-33, 56-57.

Nutt, Steven, and Josh Lyons. *Virtual Worlds and Terrorist Attack Planning.* Shawnee, OK: Urban Warfare Analysis Center, 2008.

Oakley, David. "Taming the Rogue Elephant?" *American Intelligence Journal*, 2009: 61-67.

Oatman, Robert L. *Executive Protection: New Solutions for a New Era.* Arnold, Maryland: Noble House, 2006.

O'Neill, Bard E. *Armed Struggle in Palestine: A Political-Military Analysis.* Boulder: Westview Press, 1978.

Paladin Press. *Federal Bomb Intelligence: U.S. Government Guide to Terrorist Explosives.* Boulder: Paladin Press, 1991.

—. *Handbook for Volunteers of the Irish Republican Army.* Boulder, CO: Paladin Press, 1985.

—. *KGB Alpha Team Training Manual: How the Soviets Trained for Personal Combat, Assassination, and Subversion.* Boulder: Paladin Press, 1993.

Pelton, Robert Young. *Licensed to Kill: Hired Guns in the War on Terror.* New York: Three Rivers Press, 2007.

Peters, Ralph. "Killing with Kindness: Political correctness infiltrates the Army." *Armed Forces Journal*, December 2006: 28-32.

—. "Rebels and Religion: How fighters become fanatics." *Armed Forces Journal*, January 2007: 28-31.

—. "When Muslim armies won: Lessons from yesteryears's jihadi victories." *Armed Forces Journal*, September 2007: 38-41,47.

Phalen, D.J. "Protecting Those Who Save Lives." *The Journal of Counterterrorism & Homeland Security International* 17, no. 2 (2011): 24-26.

Plaster, John L. *Secret Commandos: Behind Enemy Lines with the Elite Warriors of SOG.* New York: Simon and Schuster, 2004.

Poole, H. John. *Dragon Days: Time for "Unconventional" Tactics.* Emerald Isle, NC: Posterity Press, 2007.

—. *Global Warrior: Averting WWIII.* Emerald Isle, NC: Posterity Press, 2011.

—. *Militant Tricks: Battlefield Ruses of the Islamic Insurgent.* Emerald Isle, North Carolina: Posterity Press, 2005.

—. *Tactics of the Crescent Moon: Militant Muslim Combat Methods.* Emerald Isle, North Carolina: Posterity Press, 2004.

—. *Tequila Junction: 4th-Generation Counterinsurgency.* Emerald Isle, NC: Posterity Press, 2008.

—. *The Tiger's Way: A U.S. Private's Best Chance for Survival.* Emerald Isle, NC: Posterity Press, 2003.

Povlock, Paul A. "A Guerrilla War At Sea: The Sri Lankan Civil War." *Small Wars Journal.* Small Wars Foundation, September 9, 2011.

Powers Jr., James F. *Filling Special Operations Gaps with Civilian Expertise.* JSOU Report 07-1, Hurlburt Field: Joint Special Operations University, 2006.

Purpura, Philip P. *Security and loss prevention: An introduction.* 5th. Burlington, MA: Elsevier Butterworth-Heinemann, 2008.

Rabinovich, Abraham. *The Yom Kippur War: The Epic Encounter that Transformed the Middle East.* New York: Schocken, 2004.

Rambaud, Alfred. *The History of Russia: From the Earliest Times to 1877.* Vol. I. New York: John B. Alden, 1886.

Randal, Jonathan. *Osama: The Making of a Terrorist.* New York: Vintage Books, 2004.

Rasell, Edith. *Social Security and Medicare: Examining Proposed "Reforms".* Policy Paper, Grand Rapids: Justice & Witness Ministries, UCC, 2009.

Rashid, Ahmed. *Taliban: Militant Islam, Oil and Fundamentalism in Central Asia.* Second. New Haven, CT: Yale University Press, 2010.

Rassler, Don, and Vahid Brown. *The Haqqani Nexis and the Evolution of al-Qa'ida.* U.S. Army Harmony Program, United States Military Academy, West Point: The Combating Terrorism Center at West Point, 2011.

Ratner, Steven R. "Predator and Prey: Seizing and Killing Suspected Terrorists Abroad." *The Journal of Political Philosophy* 15, no. 3 (2007): 251-275.

Directed by Pierre Rehov. Produced by Pierre Rehov. 2006.

Reisman, W. Michael, and Chris T. Antoniou. *The Laws of War: A comprehensive collection of primary documents on international laws governing armed conflict.* New York: Random House, 1994.

Richelson, Jeffrey T. *A Century of Spies: Intelligence in the twentieth century.* New York: Oxford University Press, 1995.

—. *The U.S. Intelligence Community.* Fifth Edition. Boulder: Westview Press, 2008.

Rooney, David. *Guerrilla: Insurgents, patriots, and terrorists from Sun Tzu to Bin Laden.* London: Brassey's, 2004.

Ross, John F. *War on the Run: The Epic Story of Robert Rogers and the Conquest of America's First Frontier.* New York: Bantam Books, 2009.

Roston, Aram. "Update: SOUTHCOM ISR helped kill 'narco-terrorists'." *C4ISR Journal,* June 2013: 8.

Sawyer, Ralph D., trans. *The Seven Military Classics of Ancient China.* Boulder: Westview Press, 1993.

Schroen, Gary C. *First In: An Isider's Account of How the CIA Spearheaded the War on Terror in Afghanistan.* New York: Ballantine Books, 2007.

Shulsky, Abram N., and Gary J. Schmitt. *Silent Warfare: Understanding the World of Intelligence.* Third Edition. Washington: Potomac Books, 2002.

Shultz Jr., Richard H. "Showstoppers: Nine Reasons Why We Never Sent Our Special Operations Forces after al Qaeda before 9/11." In *Terrorism and Counterterrorism: Understanding the New Security Environment: Readings and Interpretations,* by Russell D., Sawyer, Reid L. Howard, 518-530. Dubuque, IA: McGraw-Hill, 2006.

Silinsky, Mark. "A Briefing Yet to Be Delivered: Islamism and the U.S. Defense Intelligence Community." *American Intelligence Journal* 28, no. 1 (2010): 160-163.

Simpson, Christopher. *Science of Coercion: Communications Research & Psychological Warfare 1945-1960.* New York: Oxford University Press, 1994.

Singer, Saul. "Breaking the spell of global fatalism." *The Jerusalem Post,* June 6, 2008: 4.

Sinno, Abdulkader H. *Organizations at War in Afghanistan and Beyond.* Ithaca, NY: Cornell University Press, 2008.

Sloan, Stephen, and Robert J. Bunker. *Red Teams and Counterterrorism Training.* Norman, OK: University of Oklahoma Press, 2011.

Smith, Adam C., David B. Skarbek, and Bart J. Wilson. "Anarchy, groups, and conflict: an experiment on the emergence of protective associations." *Social Choice & Welfare* 38, no. 2 (February 2012): 325-353.

Smith, Jim. *A Law Enforcement and Security Officers' Guide to Responding to Bomb Threats.* Second. Springfield, IL: Charles C. Thomas, 2009.

Sockut, Eugene. *Secrets of Street Survival -- Israeli Style: Staying alive in a Civilian War Zone.* Boulder: Paladin Press, 1995.

Spalding, Robert. *Drug Subs: The Worldwide Invasion by the Narco-Submarine Fleet.* Signal Mountain, TN: Spalding Publishing, 2010.

Spencer, Robert. *The Truth about Muhammad: Founder of the World's Most Intolerant Religion.* Washington: Regnery Publishing, 2006.

Sperry, Paul. *Infiltration: How Muslim Spies and Subversives have Penetrated Washington.* Nashville: Nelson Current, 2005.

Spicer, Mark. "Mexican Drug Cartels: The Growing Threat of the Sniper Attack." *Journal of Counterterrorism & Homeland Security International* 16, no. 4 (2011): 48-50.

Sprinzak, Ehud. "The psychopolitical formation of extreme left terrorism in a democracy: The case of the Weathermen." In *Origins of Terrorism: Psychologies, Ideologies, Theologies, States of Mind*, by Walter Reich, 65-85. Washington: Woodrow Wilson Center Press, 1998.

Spulak Jr., Robert G. *A Theory of Special Operations: The Origin, Qualities, and Use of SOF.* JSOU Report 07-7, Hurlburt Field: Joint Special Operations University, 2007.

Steele, Robert D. *Human Intelligence: All Humans, All Minds, All the Time.* Carlisle, PA: Strategic Studies Institute, 2010.

Stojkovic, Stan, David Kalinich, and John Klofas. *Criminal Justice Organizations: Administration and Management.* Fifth Edition. Belmont, CA: Wadsworth, 2012.

Stoll, Cliff. *The Cuckoo's Egg: Tracking a spy through the maze of computer espionage.* New York: Pocket Books, 1990.

Sullivan, John P., and Adam Elkus. "Narco-Armor in Mexico." *Small Wars Journal*, July 2011.

Summers Jr, Harry G. *On Strategy: A Critical Analysis of the Vietnam War.* New York: Presidio Press, 1982.

Swanson, Scott. "Viral Targeting of the IED Social Network System." *Small Wars Journal*, May 2007: 2-16.

Taber, Robert. *War of the Flea: The Classic Study of Guerrilla Warfare.* Washington: Potomac Books, 2002.

Terrill, W. Andrew. *The Saudi-Iranian Rivalry and the Future of Middle East Security.* Carlisle, PA: Strategic Studies Institute, 2011.

Thomas, Evan. *The Very Best Men: The Daring Early Years of the CIA.* New York: Simon & Schuster, 2006.

Thomas, Timothy L. "Russian Tactical Lessons Learned Fighting Chechen Separatists." *Journal of Slavic Military Studies*, 2005: 731-766.

Thornton, Rod. *Organizational Change in the Russian Airborne Forces: The Lessons of the Georgian Conflict.* Carlisle, PA: Strategic Studies Institute, 2011.

Thurman, James T. *Practical Bomb Scene Investigation.* Boca Raton, FL: CRC Press, 2006.

Tomajczyk, Stephen. F. *Bomb Squads.* Osceola, WI: MBI Publishing, 1999.

Toolis, Kevin. *Rebel Hearts: Journeys Within the IRA's Soul.* New York: St. Martin's Griffin, 1995.

Truesdell, Matthew. *Spectacular Politics: Louis-Napoleon Bonaparte and the Fete Imperiale, 1849-1870.* New York City: Oxford University Press, 1997.

Tse-tung, Mao. *On Guerrilla Warfare.* New York: Classic House Books, 2009.

Tucker, David. "Fighting Barbarians." *Parameters*, Summer 1998: 69-79.

Tucker, Johathan B. *War of Nerves: Chemical Warfare from World War I to Al-Qaeda.* New York: Pantheon, 2006.

Turbiville Jr., Graham H. *Hunting Leadership Targets in Counterinsurgency and Counterterrorist Operations: Selected Perspectives and Experiences.* JSOU Report 07-6, Hurlbert Field: Joint Special Operations University, 2007.

U.S. Army Training and Doctrine Command. *A Military Guide to Terrorism in the Twenty-First Century.* Army Handbook, Fort Leavenworth: Deputy Chief of Staff for Intelligence, 2003.

United States Army. *FMI 3-34.119 Improvised Explosive Device Defeat.* Fort Leonard Wood: Department of the Army, 2005.

United States Catholic Conference, Inc. *Catechism of the Catholic Church.* New York: Doubleday, 1994.

United States Department of Homeland Security. *Terrorist Weaponization of Fire: Improvised Incendiary Devices (IID) and Arson.* Unclassified/For Official Use Only, Office of Intelligence, Transportation Security Administration, Washington: U.S. Government, 2008.

United States Department of the Army. *FM 31-21 Guerrilla Warfare and Special Forces Operations.* Field Manual, Washington: U.S. War Office, 1961.

United States Marine Corps. *FRONT-LINE INTELLIGENCE.* Field Manual FMFRP 12-16, Washington: Department of the Navy, 1988.

Utley, Robert L. "Crook and Miles, Fighting and Feuding on the Indian Frontier." *MHQ: The Quarterly Journal of Military History*, Autumn 1989: 81-91.

Vacca, John R. *Computer Forensics: Computer Crime Scene Investigation.* Hingham, MA: Charles River Media, Inc., 2002.

Velocity, Max. *Rapid Fire! Tactics for High Threat, Protection and Combat Operations.* Lexington, KY: Max Velocity, 2012.

Venter, Al J. *Allah's Bomb: The Islamic Quest for Nuclear Weapons.* Guilford, CT: The Lyons Press, 2007.

—. *War Dog: Fighting Other People's Wars: The Modern Mercenary in Combat.* Drexel Hill, PA: Casemate Publishing, 2008.

Waisberg, Tatiana. "The Colombia-Ecuador Armed Crisis of March 2008: The Practice of Targeted Killing and Incursions against Non-State Actors Harbored at Terrorist Safe Havens in a Third Party State." *Studies in Conflict & Terrorism* 32 (2009): 476-488.

Waller, Douglas C. *The Commandos: The inside story of America's secret soldiers.* New York: Simon & Schuster, 1994.

Watkins, Lance J. *Self-propelled Semi-submersibles: The Next Great Threat to Regional Security and Stability.* Thesis, Monterey: Naval Post-Graduate School, 2011.

Waugh, Billy, and Tim Keown. *Hunting the Jackal.* New York: Avon Books, 2004.

West, John. *Fry the Brain: The Art of Urban Sniping and its Role in Modern Guerrilla Warfare.* Countryside, VA: SSI, 2008.

Wilkinson, Paul. *Terrorism & the Liberal State.* Second Edition. New York: New York University Press, 1986.

Williams, Phil. *Criminals, Militias, and Insurgents: Organized Crime in Iraq.* Carlisle, PA: Strategic Studies Institute, 2009.

Williams, Phil. "Transnational Criminal Networks." In *Networks and Netwars: The Future of Terror, Crime, and Militancy*, edited by John Arquilla and David Ronfeldt, 61-97. Santa Monica, California: RAND Corporation, 2001.

Williams, Phil, and Vanda Felbab-Brown. *Drug Trafficking, Violence, and Instability.* Carlisle, PA: Strategic Studies Institute, 2012.

Wilson, Derek. *Charlemagne.* New York: Doubleday, 2006.

Wimberley, Scott. *Special Forces Guerrilla Warfare Manual.* Boulder: Paladin Press, 1997.

Zuhur, Sherifa. *HAMAS and ISRAEL: Conflicting Strategies of Group-Based Politics.* Carlisle, PA: Strategic Studies Institute, 2008.

# AUTHOR'S BIOGRAPHY

R.J. Godlewski (GOD LESS KEY) is currently the manager of Tactical Extractions, LLC., a threat resolution services company, and serves as president of Roadsailor Security Corporation. He is a graduate of American Military University, holding an M.A. in Military Studies, Asymmetrical Warfare concentration and a B.A. in Intelligence Studies, Terrorism Studies concentration, both earned with academic honors. He further holds graduate and undergraduate certificates in Security Management and Explosive Ordnance Disposal, respectively. Mr. Godlewski is a veteran of both the U.S. Navy and U.S. Navy Reserve.

www.ingramcontent.com/pod-product-compliance
Lightning Source LLC
Chambersburg PA
CBHW060518290526
45791CB00001B/440